Basic Microsoft Office XP skills

WITHDRAWN FROM SWINDON LIBRARIES

Jim Gatenby

BERNARD BABANI (publishing) LTD
The Grampians
Shepherds Bush Road
London W6 7NF
England

Please Note

Although every care has been taken with the production of this book to ensure that any projects, designs, modifications and/or programs, etc., contained herewith, operate in a correct and safe manner and also that any components specified are normally available in Great Britain, the Publishers and Author do not accept responsibility in any way for the failure (including fault in design) of any project, design, modification or program to work correctly or to cause damage to any equipment that it may be connected to or used in conjunction with, or in respect of any other damage or injury that may be so caused, nor do the Publishers accept responsibility in any way for the failure to obtain specified components.

Notice is also given that if equipment that is still under warranty is modified in any way or used or connected with home-built equipment then that warranty may be void.

© 2001 BERNARD BABANI (publishing) LTD

First Published - December 2001

British Library Cataloguing in Publication Data:

A catalogue record for this book is available from the British Library

Cover Design by Gregor Arthur

Printed and bound in Great Britain by The Guernsey Press

Swindon Borough Council
Library Services

Askews	
005.369	£6.99

About this Book

Microsoft Office XP contains everything the student or the home or business user needs to manage their affairs, from the essential office software of word processor, spreadsheet and database to the tools needed for using the Internet. Office XP builds on the success of earlier versions of Microsoft Office; Several new features such as Smart Tags and Task Panes make the software even more powerful yet easy to learn and use.

This book is aimed at the new user wishing to become competent with business software, perhaps with a view to improving employment opportunities. The student or professional needing to produce high quality reports will find a wealth of desktop publishing features, enabling long documents (such as this book) to be produced with ease. The small business or home user wishing to automate their accounts and records will find the spreadsheet, database and chart/graphing software very simple to use, while containing advanced features to satisfy the most demanding professional user. Anyone who acquires the basic skills with Microsoft Office XP should be well prepared to cope with the use of computers in the most sophisticated modern office.

This book concentrates on the basic skills to enable you to create solutions to a wide range of problems. Each major topic is explained in simple language, based around a familiar, everyday example. This is followed by practical "hands on" exercises designed to reinforce the previous notes. Skills checklists at the end of each section allow you to assess your progress and revise topics if necessary.

> **The first part of this book covers many of the skills required for the popular CLAIT and IBT II computer literacy courses, from Oxford Cambridge and RSA Examinations. The last chapter covers the integration of extracts from the database, spreadsheet and charting programs to form a multi-page word processed document, as required by the IBT II course. The last chapter also includes additional notes describing many of the requirements of the IBT II course.**

About the Author

Jim Gatenby trained as a Chartered Mechanical Engineer and initially worked at Rolls-Royce Ltd using computers in the analysis of performance. He obtained a Master of Philosophy degree in Mathematical Education by research at Loughborough University of Technology and has taught mathematics and computing to 'A' Level since 1972. His most recent posts have included Head of Computer Studies and Information Technology Coordinator. During this time he has written many books in the fields of educational computing and Microsoft Windows.

The author has considerable experience of teaching the use of software packages such as Microsoft Office, on which this book is based, to students of all ages and abilities, in school and in adult education. For several years he successfully taught the well-established CLAIT course (Computer Literacy and Information Technology) from Oxford Cambridge and RSA Examinations, as well as GCSE and National Curriculum Information Technology courses requiring competence in the use of software packages.

Trademarks

Microsoft Office 2000, Windows, AutoSum, Word, and Excel are trademarks or registered trademarks of Microsoft Corporation. All other brand and product names are recognised as trademarks, or registered trademarks, of their respective companies.

Acknowledgements

The author and publishers would like to thank Oxford Cambridge and RSA Examinations for permission to describe the CLAIT and Integrated Business Technology Stage II (IBT II) courses and to reproduce the Assessment Objectives for CLAIT and IBT II.

Contents

1

Introducing Office XP — 1

Microsoft Word 2002	2
Microsoft Excel 2002	3
Charts and Graphs	3
Microsoft Access 2002	4
Integration	5
New Features in Microsoft Office XP	6
Smart Tags	6
The Task Pane	8
The Windows Operating System	10
Mouse Operations	13
Working with Windows	14
Displaying Several Windows Simultaneously	16
Dialogue Boxes	17
Windows Explorer	18
Folders and Files	18
Creating a New Folder	19
Managing Files and Folders in Explorer	20
Deleting a File or Folder	21
Copying and Moving Files and Folders	22
Renaming a File or Folder	23
Creating a Shortcut	23
Finding a File	24

2

Using Microsoft Word 2002 — 25

Introduction	25
Word Processing in Context	26
Getting Started with Word 2002	27
Features of the Word 2002 Screen	28
Entering Text	30

The AutoCorrect Button	31
Saving Your Work	32
The AutoRecover Feature and Automatic Saving	33
Exercise 1 - Entering and Saving Text	35
Editing Text	36
Retrieving a File from Disc	36
Keys Used for Editing Text	37
Block Operations	38
The Clipboard Task Pane	40
The Paste Options Button	41
Checking the Spelling	42
Find and Replace	43
Printing Your Work	44
Exercise 2 - Editing and Printing	45
Changing the Format and Layout	46
Changing the Page Margins	46
Indenting Paragraphs	47
Changing Line Spacing	48
Changing the Measurement Units	48
Applying Formatting Effects	49
Exercise 3 - Changing the Format and Layout	50
Keyboard Shortcuts	51
Exercise 4 - All Basic Word Processing Skills	52
Checklist of CLAIT Word Processing Skills	54

3

Using Microsoft Access 2002   55

Introduction	55
Designing the Record Structure	57
Creating a Database in Access	58
Saving and Editing the Record Structure	61
Entering the Data	63
Saving a Table	64
Exercise 5 - Creating a Database File	65

Editing a Previously Saved File	66
Exercise 6 - Editing a Database File	70
Retrieving Information	71
Queries - Sorting and Searching a File	71
Saving a Query	78
Printing a Query	78
Exercise 7 - Manipulating a Database File	79
Exercise 8 - All Basic Database Skills	80
Checklist of CLAIT Database Skills	82
Creating a Form	83
Creating a Report	87

4

Using Microsoft Excel 2002   89

Introduction	89
Getting Started with Excel 2002	91
Moving Around in a Spreadsheet	92
Cell Contents	93
Labels	93
Numbers	94
Formulae	94
Totalling Rows and Columns	95
Functions	96
Creating a Spreadsheet	97
Entering Labels	97
Entering Numbers	97
Entering Formulae	98
Replication	98
Saving a Spreadsheet File	99
Printing a Spreadsheet	99
Displaying and Printing Formulae	99
Exercise 9 - Creating a Spreadsheet	101
Editing a Spreadsheet	102

Replicating a Formula Down a Column	104
Auto Fill Options	105
Deleting Rows and Columns	106
Inserting Rows and Columns	107
Exercise 10 - Editing a Spreadsheet	109
Formatting a Spreadsheet	110
Numbers in Decimal Format	113
Numbers in Integer Format	114
Exercise 11 - Formatting a Spreadsheet	115
Exercise 12 - All Basic Spreadsheet Skills	116
Checklist of CLAIT Spreadsheet Skills	118

5

Graphs and Charts

	119
Introduction	119
The Pie Chart	120
The Bar Chart	120
The Comparative Bar Chart	121
The Line Graph and Comparative Line Graph	121
Creating a Pie Chart	122
Selecting Two Columns Simultaneously	122
Using the Chart Wizard	123
Printing and Saving a Chart	126
Modifying an Existing Chart	127
Exercise 13 - Creating a Pie Chart	128
Creating a Bar Chart	129
Changing the Patterns of the Bars	131
The Comparative Bar Chart	132
Exercise 14 - Creating a Bar Chart	134
Creating a Line Graph	135
Changing the Size of a Chart or Graph	137
Exercise 15 - Basic Graphical Representation of Data Skills	138
Checklist of CLAIT Graphical Representation Skills	141

6

Further Work with Word 2002 — 143

Introduction	143
Setting the Margins	144
Line Length	144
Indentation	145
Paper Size	146
Changing Character Size	146
Numbering the Pages	147
Page Breaks	148
Tabulation	149
Inserting Tables	151
Hiding Gridlines	152
Bullets and Numbering	152

7

Creating an Integrated Document — 153

Introduction	153
Multitasking	153
Inserting a Spreadsheet into a Word Document	155
Inserting a Graph or Chart into a Word Document	159
Inserting a Database Extract into a Word Document	163
Working with Pictures	166
Inserting a Graphic into a Word Document	166
Inserting a Picture from a File	168
Moving a Graphic and Setting Text Wrapping	169
Additional Notes for the IBT II Course	170
Checklist of Skills for IBT II	177

Index — 179

1
Introducing Office XP

Microsoft Office XP

Office XP is a collection of several computer programs that together enable all of the main office tasks to be carried out. In computing jargon, it's known as an *integrated software package*. All of the different component programs making up the package are designed to work with each other and are supplied on a single CD.

Advantages of integrated software packages such as Office XP are:

- All of the programs work in the same way, with similar menus and commands, making them easier to learn and use.
- It's easy to transfer data between the different programs.

Microsoft Office XP contains a large *suite* of programs for a variety of tasks; this book concentrates on the basic core tools, word processor, spreadsheet, database and charts and graphs. These programs, known as *applications,* can easily be launched from the **Microsoft Office Shortcut Bar**, as shown below.

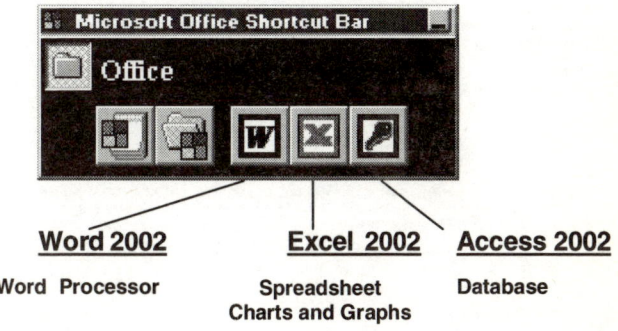

1   Introducing Office XP

There are two different packages to choose from, Microsoft Office XP Standard and Microsoft Office XP Professional. Office XP Professional contains all of the programs you need to follow the work in this book. Microsoft Office XP Standard does not include the Access database, which is an important part of the work both in this book and on computer literacy courses in general.

Word, Excel and Access are widely used for CLAIT and IBT II, the popular courses from Oxford Cambridge and RSA Examinations, recognised by many employers as evidence of computer literacy.

The exercises in this book should help you acquire basic skills with Office XP and are also compatible with the CLAIT and IBT II courses.

Microsoft Word 2002

This is the leading word processing program in the office, in education and in the home. Word can be used to produce any sort of text-based document including memos and letters, magazines and student projects or complex reports containing tables, pictures and graphs. You can also use Word to prepare the text of an e-mail or a Web page for the Internet. Numerous Desktop publishing effects are available such as different styles of lettering and text in newspaper-style columns. Word can even be used to typeset full size books (such as this one).

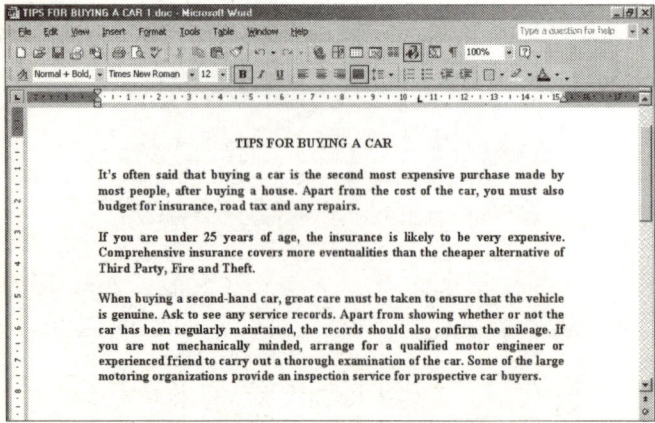

Introducing Office XP 1

Microsoft Excel 2002

Excel is a leading spreadsheet program, used wherever tables of figures have to be calculated. It's often used to prepare sales figures and accounts in business but can equally be used, for example, to process the results of surveys and experiments. Programs like Excel save many hours of work compared with traditional methods. Rows and columns of figures can be calculated effortlessly and recalculated to predict future trends, such as "What if prices rise at 5%?"

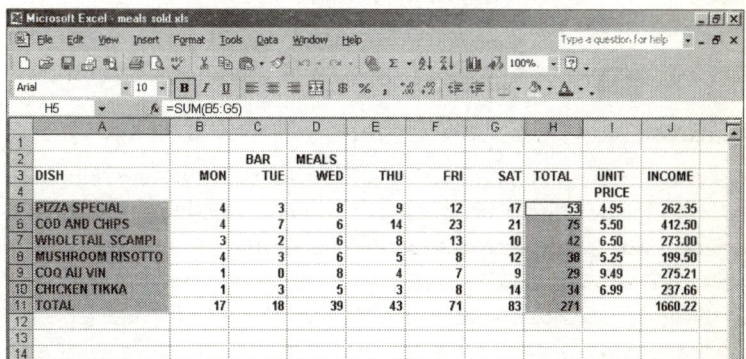

Charts and Graphs

The Excel 2002 spreadsheet program includes a powerful charting facility. This enables, for example, line graphs, bar charts and pie charts to be drawn in a variety of styles, incorporating headings, labels, colours and shading.

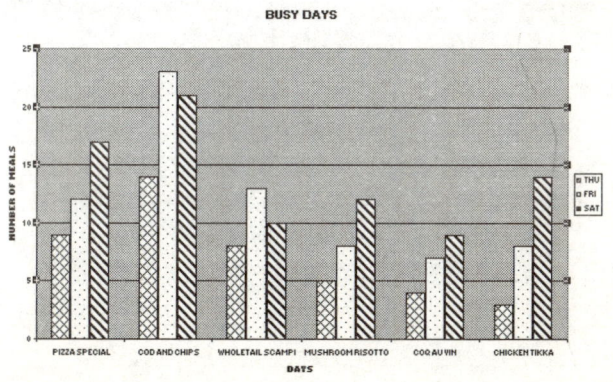

1 Introducing Office XP

Microsoft Access 2002

Microsoft Access 2002 is a database program. A database *file* is a set of similar records, such as a list of cars for sale, as shown below.

The computer database may be contrasted with traditional methods of keeping records on cards. The computer records may be *searched* far more quickly to find particular records or *sorted* into alphabetical or numerical order with one click of the mouse. Computer records can easily be *updated* by adding new records or by amending or deleting existing records. In *table view*, as shown below, each record is one row across the table.

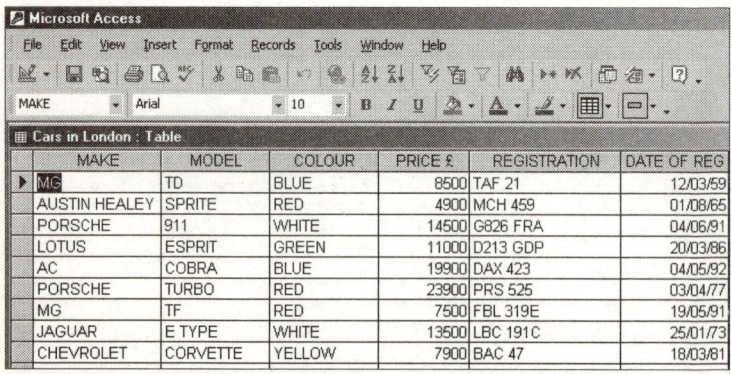

In *form view* the records appear on the screen one at a time, as shown below. You can alter the design of the form with desktop publishing effects such as different styles of lettering, colours and graphics.

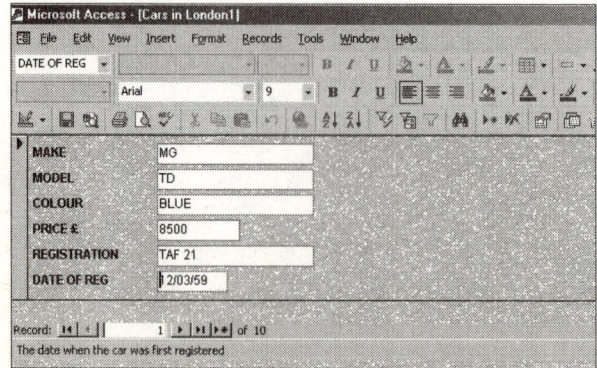

Integration

As mentioned previously, Office XP is an integrated software package or *suite* of programs. The individual Office XP programs are designed to exchange data with each other. This may not be the case when using a mixture of programs obtained from a variety of different software manufacturers.

When producing a business or technical report, you would create the text of the report in a word processor and import extracts from other programs such as spreadsheet, database and graphics.

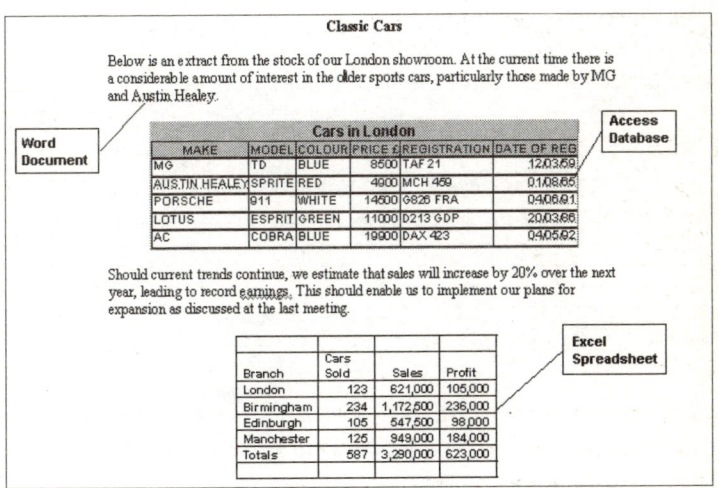

This exchange of data is achieved by copying the required extract from the originating program then "pasting" it into the Word document. The process is described in more detail later in this book.

Taking extracts of data from several different programs and incorporating them into a single document is part of the Integrated Business Technology Stage II course from Oxford Cambridge and RSA Examinations. The work on integration later in this book, although intended for all users of Office XP, should also be very relevant to students preparing for the IBT II certificate.

1 Introducing Office XP

New Features in Microsoft Office XP

Office XP is the latest edition in a series of Microsoft Office packages, including Microsoft Office 97 and Microsoft Office 2000. If you have used one of these earlier versions, then you will find the familiar features are still present. However, Microsoft Office XP (its name derived from e**XP**erience) introduces a wealth of new features intended to make the software more powerful and yet easier to use. The next few pages discuss the new Office XP features which are particularly relevant within the context of this book.

Smart Tags

Suppose, while you are entering text into the Word 2002 word processor, you make a mistake in the spelling of a common word or make incorrect use of capital letters. The AutoCorrect feature in Office XP automatically changes the text to the conventional spelling or changes to the normal use of upper and lower case letters. In the example below, the word "you" was incorrectly entered as "yuo".

> While you are typing, if you make a mistake in a common word, the AutoCorrect feature in Word 2002 will automatically make a correction. Then you are
>
>   Change back to "yuo"
>   Stop Automatically Correcting "yuo"
>   Control AutoCorrect Options...

In this example, the AutoCorrect feature in Word 2002 changes "yuo" back to "you" without any intervention from the user. However, if you pass the cursor over the changed word, a small rectangle and an icon appear, as shown on the left. This is an example of a *smart tag*. On the right of the smart tag is a small down arrow. Clicking the down arrow on a smart tag leads to a menu, such as the AutoCorrect menu shown above. In this example, the smart tag menu allows you to undo the automatic correction, if the original spelling was what you really intended.

Introducing Office XP 1

If you type some text in Word or Excel, etc., and it is recognised as a name, the name is underlined in purple dots. Passing the cursor over the name reveals the **Smart Tag Actions** button shown below.

A smart tag also appears when you type a person's name such as Jean Smith, the

Clicking the down arrow on the right of the smart tag launches the menu shown on the right, allowing you to send an e-mail or arrange a meeting, for example.

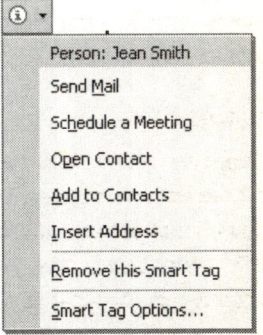

The **Smart Tag Actions** button can be set to recognise other data items in addition to the names of people. If you select **Smart Tag Options...** from the menu shown on the right, the **AutoCorrect** dialogue box opens showing the **Smart Tags** tab. Here you can add or remove items from the list of recognised types of data, as shown below.

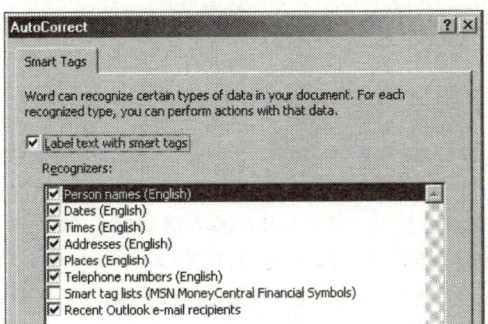

If the recognised data type is an address, for example, rather then a person's name, a different set of actions appears on the drop-down **Smart Tag Actions** menu, as shown on the right.

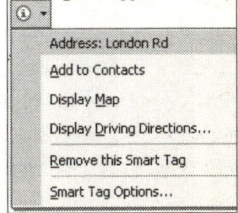

7

1 Introducing Office XP

Paste Options

When entering text in programs like Microsoft Word and Excel, it's often necessary to copy a piece of text from another document (or another part of the same document) and "paste" it into the current Word document. After pasting a piece of text in one of the Office XP programs the **Paste Options** button appears, as shown below.

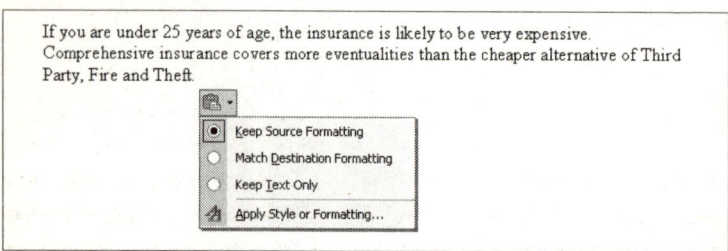

Clicking the down arrow to the right of the **Paste Options** button shows a list of formatting options. These include keeping the formatting of the original (source) document or changing to a completely new style. Cutting and pasting of extracts between the various Office XP programs is covered in more detail later in this book.

The Task Pane

The Task Pane is a window on the right of the screen which gives the user access to a wide range of features and resources, without obscuring the main window of the current application. The Task Pane is available in the main applications such as Word, Excel and Access. If the Task Pane is not currently displayed it can be launched by selecting **View** and **Task Pane** from the menu bar of the current application.

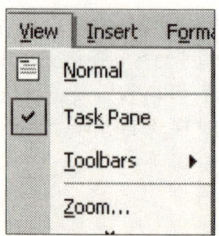

Introducing Office XP 1

The example below shows the Task Pane in Excel open at the **New Workbook** window.

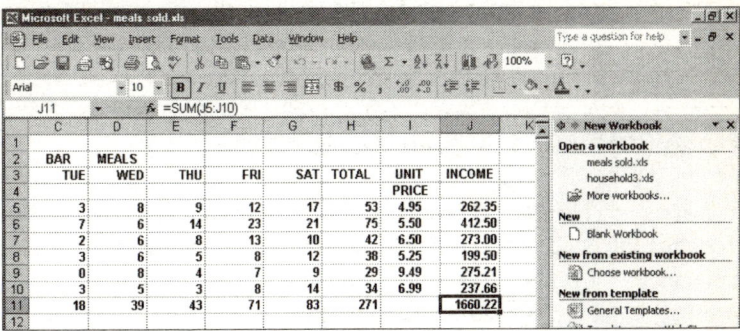

In a given application, such as Word or Excel, there are various Task Panes, allowing the user to carry out a range of tasks. Click the down arrow at the top right of the Task Pane window to view the list of Task Panes, as shown below on the right using Word 2002 as an example.

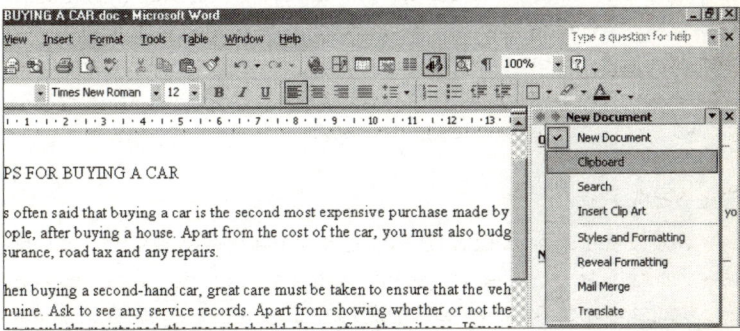

If you select **Clipboard** from the drop-down menu above, a new Task Pane appears listing all of the items which you have currently copied to the clipboard. (The clipboard is an area of memory used as a temporary store during "cutting and pasting" operations). The clipboard Task Pane is particularly useful, making it easy to see up to 24 items available for pasting into a document. Graphics stored on the clipboard are shown in the Task Pane as thumbnail images. The Task Pane is discussed in more detail later in this book.

1 Introducing Office XP

The Windows Operating System

An *operating system* is the software controlling the computer and devices like the disc drives and printers. The operating system is always working, no matter what *applications* you are running, such as Word, Excel or Access. Windows is called a *multi-tasking* operating system; this means it can run several applications at the same time.

To run Office XP, you need one of the later versions of Windows - Windows 98, Me, NT4, Windows 2000 Professional or Windows XP. Together these operating systems control most of the newer PCs sold throughout the world. In the past, Windows NT and 2000 tended to be used by larger organisations while Windows 95, 98 and Me often found favour with individual users and smaller organisations. The latest version, Windows XP, is intended to provide a single operating system suitable for all types of user.

Microsoft Windows enables you to interact with the computer through a *graphical user interface* (GUI), using small pictures or *icons*. When you start your computer the Windows Desktop opens up showing icons representing the software installed on your hard disc

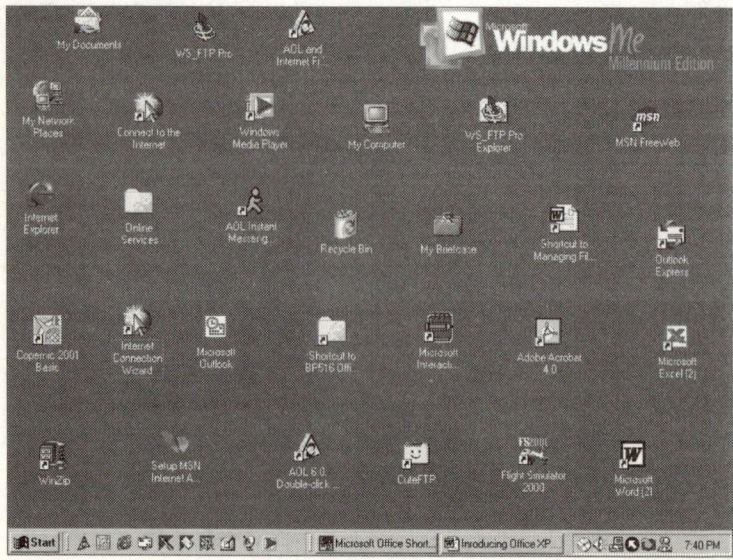

On the Windows Desktop shown previously, some of the icons represent programs provided by Windows itself, such as **My Computer** and the **Recycle Bin**. Other icons such as the one for **WinZip**, are placed on the Desktop when a new program is first installed. An easy way to launch a program is to double click its icon on the Windows Desktop. You can place icons or *shortcuts* for other programs on the Desktop, as discussed shortly.

The bar along the bottom of the Desktop is known as the *Taskbar*, described on the next page. On the left of the Taskbar is the frequently used **Start** button.

The Start Button

If an application does not have an icon on the Desktop, it is normally invoked after clicking the **Start** button. Then point to **Programs**, move across the menu and click over the required program.

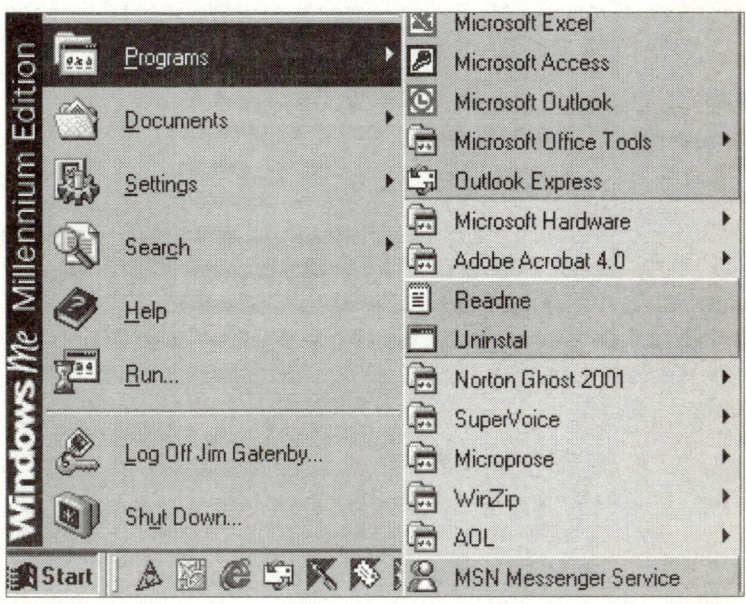

1 Introducing Office XP

The Taskbar

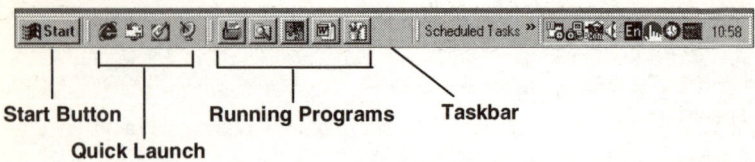

Start Button | Running Programs | Taskbar
Quick Launch

As well as the **Start** button, the Taskbar shows icons for the programs currently up and running in your computer. If you were running Word on the screen, with Excel and Paint running in the background, clicking the Excel icon on the Taskbar would switch to Excel displayed on the screen, with Word and Paint in the background.

Word Paint Excel

The Quick Launch icons, towards the left of the Taskbar, invoke Windows' own programs such as Internet Explorer, Outlook Express e-mail and the Windows Desktop. To find out what an icon represents, allow the mouse pointer to hover over the icon until an explanatory note appears.

Shutting Down Windows

After you finish work, always close down the system according to the correct procedure, described below.

N.B. <u>Do not simply switch off the power to the computer!</u>

This may damage your hard disc or cause the loss of important work. Also, the next time you start the computer you'll have to wait while Windows scans the hard disc to correct any problems caused by the incorrect shut down.

To Shut Down Safely:

- Save your work and close any programs and files that are open, by clicking the cross at the top right of the window.
- Select **Start** and **Shut Down...** off the Taskbar.
- Click **OK** and wait until the message "**It's now safe...**" appears.
- Switch off the power to the computer.

Mouse Operations

The next section "Working With Windows" shows how various objects on the Windows screen can be manipulated with the aid of the mouse. Before starting, it may be helpful to review the various mouse operations:

Click

This means a single press of the left mouse button. With the cursor over an icon or screen object, a click will cause, for example, a command from a menu to be carried out or a window to open or close.

Double Click

This means pressing the left mouse button very quickly twice in succession. This is often used to carry out operations such as starting a program from an icon on the Desktop and for opening a folder.

Right Click

Pressing the right button while the pointer is over a screen object is a quick way to open up additional menus relating to the object. For example, if you right click over the **Start** 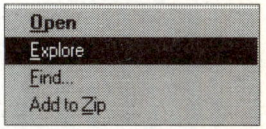 button on the Taskbar, a menu appears giving, amongst other things, a quick way to start the Windows Explorer.

Dragging and Dropping

This is used to move objects about the screen. Click over the object, then, keeping the left button held down, move the mouse pointer (together with the object) to the new position. Release the left button to place the object in its new position. Dragging is also used to resize windows and graphics on the screen.

Creating a Shortcut Icon on the Desktop

To provide a shortcut icon on the Desktop for any of your programs, from the **Start** menu, select **Programs**. *Right click* the name or icon for the program and click **Send To**. Now select **Desktop (create shortcut)** to place an icon on the Windows Desktop. From now on the program can be started by double clicking the icon on the Desktop.

1 Introducing Office XP

Working with Windows

Whenever you run a program under the Windows operating system, it appears on the screen in its own rectangular frame. These frames are known as *windows* and they are also used for displaying folders.

The manipulation of a window can be illustrated using **My Computer**, one of the main features of Windows and started by double clicking its icon on the Windows Desktop. **My Computer** is represented by a window showing all of the disc drives and other resources on your computer.

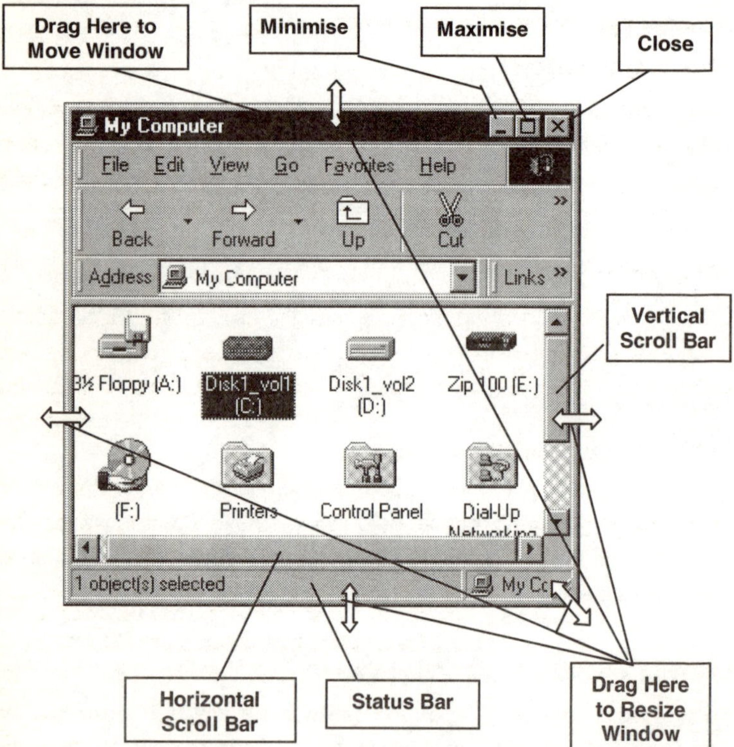

The same methods are used to work with all sorts of windows, including windows containing folders as well as windows containing programs.

Introducing Office XP

The Maximise Button

Click this to make the window fill the entire screen.

The Minimise Button

Click this to reduce the window to an icon on the Taskbar. Click the icon on the Taskbar to restore a window to its original size.

The Restore Button

After a window has been maximised, the **Maximise Button** is replaced by the **Restore Button** shown right. Clicking this reduces the window to its original size.

Resizing a Window

You can change the size of a window by dragging arrows on each of the four sides and in the corners of the window. These are shown on the window on the previous page. Move the mouse pointer over the border until the arrows appear. Then drag the border to the required size.

The Menu Bar

The Menu Bar is a list of words across the top of the window starting with **File**, **Edit** and **View**, etc. For example, the menu bar from the Word 2002 program is shown below. A single click reveals a drop-down menu, such as the **File** menu illustrated. Then the required command is executed, again with a single click.

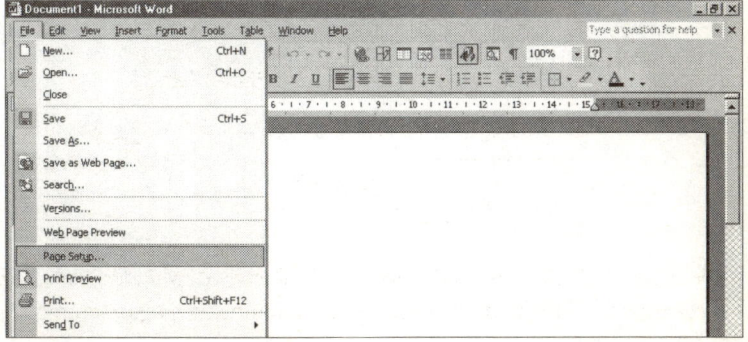

1   Introducing Office XP

Displaying Several Windows Simultaneously

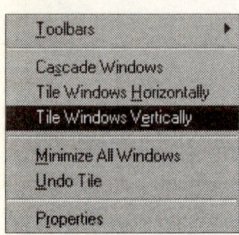

When two or more programs are running at the same time, normally only one of them is seen in a window on the screen. Microsoft Windows allows two or more windows to be displayed simultaneously by a *tiling* arrangement. Tiling is achieved after right clicking on an empty part of the Windows Taskbar at the bottom of the screen. This brings up the menu shown above left. Selecting **Tile Windows Vertically** when running Word and Excel produced the following result, for example.

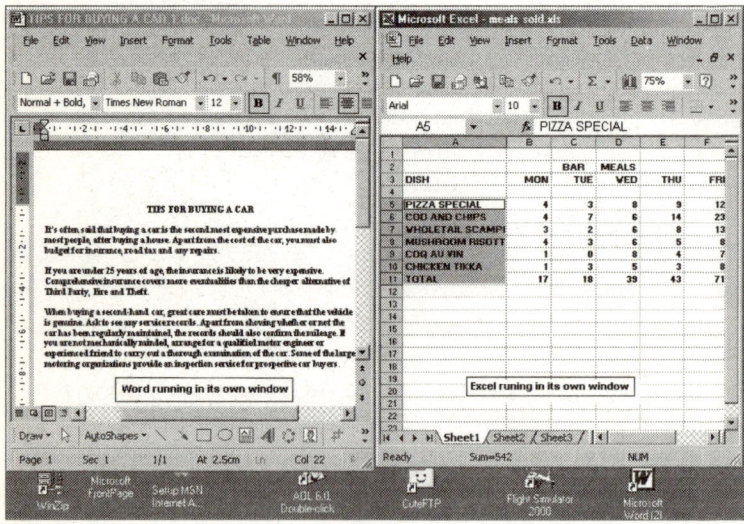

The **Cascade Windows** command shown in the menu at the top of the page has the effect of arranging the windows on top of each other in layers, but with the title bar of each window clearly visible. Clicking on the title bar of a window brings that window to the top layer. Please note that windows currently minimised on the Taskbar are not included in any tiling or cascading arrangements.

Introducing Office XP 1

Dialogue Boxes

Whereas the windows discussed previously contain running programs and folders, *dialogue boxes* usually require the user to enter information or specify settings. (Changing dialogue box settings is not compulsory, since Microsoft Windows provides *default* settings and names which will usually suffice until you are ready to insert your own.)

Dialogue boxes appear after you select a menu command which ends in an ellipsis (**...**) such as **Save As...** and **Print...**. The **Print** dialogue box shown below contains many of the most common features.

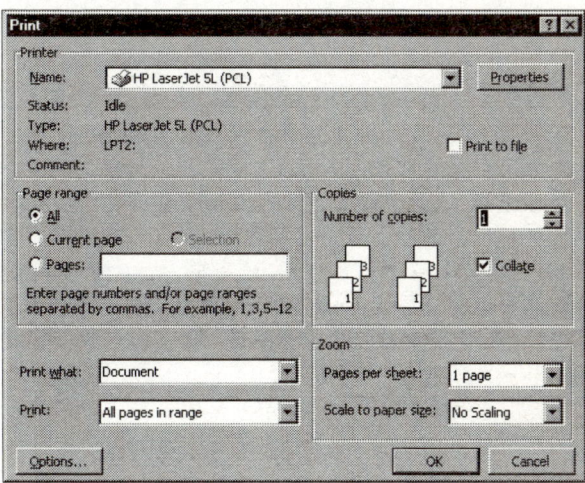

The white circles under **Page range** are known as *radio buttons*, switched on or off with a single click. Only one of a group of radio buttons can be switched on at a given time.

The white squares next to **Collate** and **Print to file** are known as *check boxes*. Any number of check boxes can be switched on or off at a given time.

Clicking the down arrow on the right of a horizontal bar reveals a *drop-down menu* of choices, such as several types of printer.

Some dialogue boxes, for example, **Save As**, have a *text box* which allows you to type in your own words, such as a file name.

1 Introducing Office XP

Windows Explorer

Explorer is a part of the Windows operating system - not to be confused with Internet Explorer, the Web browser. Throughout this book the term "Explorer" will refer to the Windows Explorer.

Explorer is a tool for organising your work. It can be invoked by clicking **Start**, **Programs**, **Accessories** and **Windows Explorer**. A quicker way is to right click over the **Start** button and click **Explore** on the menu which pops up. Explorer is shown below, in its own window.

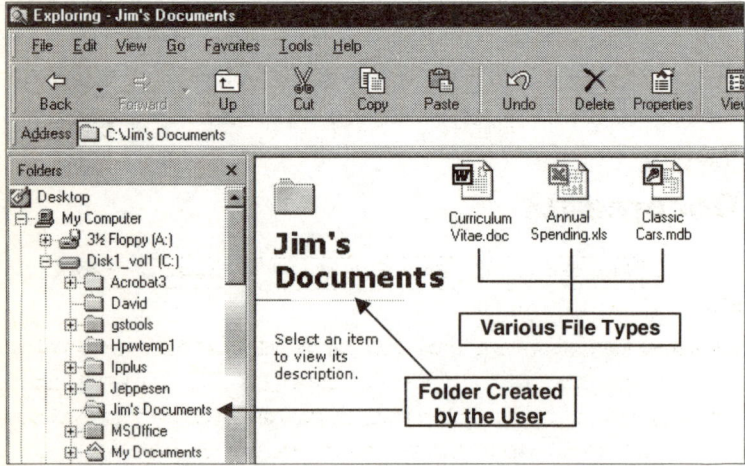

Folders and Files

All the disc drives and folders on your computer are listed in the left-hand panel of Explorer, as shown above. Some folders, such as **My Documents**, are provided by Windows by default. Others, like the **MSOffice** folder listed above, are created when you install new software. Finally, you can create folders in which to store your work, such as **Jim's Documents** above.

When a piece of work is saved in a folder it is generally referred to as a *file*. When you save your work (discussed later) you normally enter a *file name*, although Windows will supply one by default, if necessary.

Creating a New Folder

A new folder can be created as a separate entity or as a sub-folder within an existing folder. To create a new folder, in Explorer:

- Click the disc drive or folder which is to be the "home" for the new folder. It should appear highlighted in the Explorer window.
- Click **File** on the menu bar, then click **New** and **Folder**.
- Type a name for the new folder in the box which appears, replacing the words **New Folder** as shown below.
- Press **Enter** and the new folder should appear in Explorer.

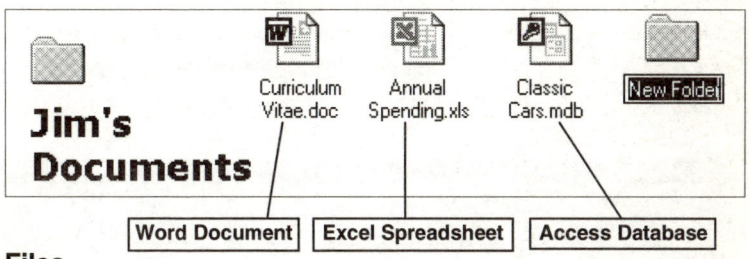

Files

In the above folder there are three files, representing a Word document, an Excel spreadsheet and an Access database file. The different types of file are identified by special icons and by the file name extensions (**.doc**, **.xls** and **.mdb**) which Windows adds when the file is saved.

Creating Sub-folders

You can create a new folder either as a standalone entity on a disc drive or as a subfolder within an existing folder. This leads to a tree-like hierarchy of folders, as shown right. The folder **Jim's Documents** is at the highest level on drive **C:**. **Business** and **Leisure** are subfolders of **Jim's Documents**. **Excel**, **Access** and **Word** are subfolders of **Business**.

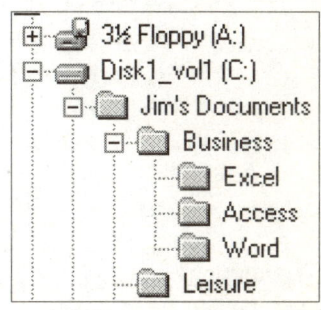

Managing Files and Folders in Explorer

Although files and folders appear to be quite different types of object, they are managed in the same way in Explorer. (*Managing* here means routine tasks like copying, moving, deleting and renaming).

There are usually several alternative methods of carrying out a given task in Microsoft Windows. The methods described on the following pages are considered to be relatively straightforward.

Please Note:

Although the following notes are based on managing files, the operations described can generally be used with folders.

Several important tasks can be accomplished by *right* clicking over a file's icon in the Windows Explorer. A drop-down menu appears, as shown below. The menu contains several file management commands.

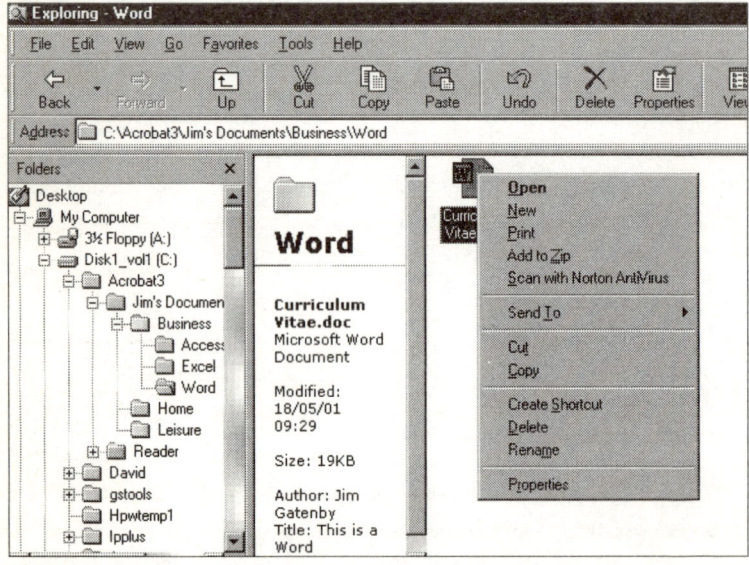

The functions of some of the main commands on the above menu are described on the following pages.

Introducing Office XP 1

Deleting a File or Folder

From the drop-down menu as shown on the previous page, click **Delete**. The file disappears from Explorer but it's simply sent to another folder on the hard disc, called the **Recycle Bin**. You are given the chance to cancel the **Delete** operation with the question **"Are you your sure ..."**.

The Recycle Bin

Files sent to the **Recycle Bin** are still present on your hard disc. To get rid of them completely you must empty the Recycle Bin. Open the Recycle Bin by double-clicking its icon on the Windows Desktop.

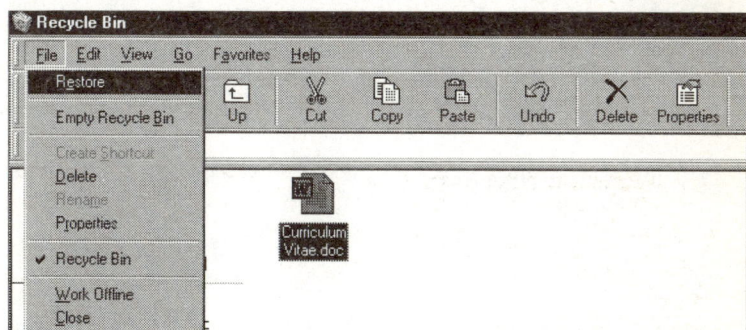

If you highlight a file in the Recycle Bin, the **File** menu shown above gives you the chance to **Restore** the file to its original folder. Selecting **Empty Recycle Bin** permanently deletes the file.

Alternatively, right click over the file's icon in the Recycle Bin to bring up the menu shown right. Now select **Restore** to reinstate the file in its original folder or select **Delete** to get rid of the file for good.

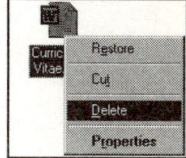

The Recycle Bin should be emptied regularly, particularly if you running out of space on the hard disc. Files in the Recycle Bin are still occupying disc space. Lack of disc space causes some programs to run slowly and others not to run at all.

1 Introducing Office XP

Copying and Moving Files and Folders

These two similar tasks can be carried out in the Windows Explorer. In general, notes referring to files can also be applied to folders.

Copying a File

This operation is typically carried out in order to:

- Make a further or *backup* copy of a file for security reasons.
- Place a copy of a file on a floppy disc or other medium, so that it can be taken away and used on another computer.

Moving a File

This deletes a file from its original location and should be used with great care. Typically used to move your *work files* about the hard disc in order to organise them into a hierarchy of folders.

Method

- In Explorer, right click over the file or folder and keep the right button held down.
- Drag the file to the disc or folder in which it is to be placed and release the right button. A menu opens as shown below.
- Left click either **Move Here** or **Copy Here** to complete the process.

N.B. Never attempt to move files or folders which are part of the Windows operating system or files which are part of applications such as Word 2002, Access 2002 or Excel 2002.

Introducing Office XP

Renaming a File or Folder

Right click over the file in Explorer and select **Rename** from the drop-down menu (shown on page 20). The name of the file appears in a frame with a cursor, ready to change the file name. When typing in the new file name, you need to add the file name extension e.g. **.doc**, **.xls** or **.mdb**. Otherwise the **Rename** box shown below will appear, to which you should answer **No**.

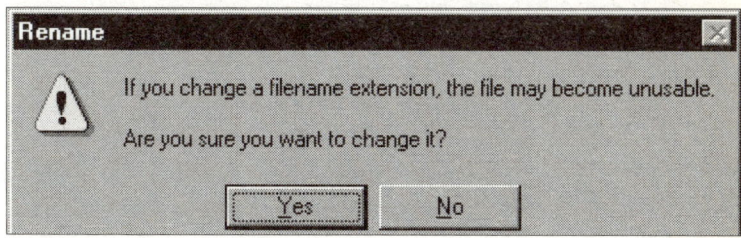

Creating a Shortcut

If you are regularly working on a file, you can create a short cut icon for the file on the Windows Desktop. To create a shortcut, right click over the file in Explorer then select **Create Shortcut** from the menu (shown on page 20). A shortcut icon is created in the Explorer panel.

Now drag this icon and drop it over **Desktop** in the left-hand Explorer panel shown above. You can also use **Send To** and **Desktop (create shortcut)**.

This places the icon on the Desktop. To open the file at the start of a session, double click the icon on the Windows Desktop. In this example, the **Excel** program will start up with the file **annual spending.xls** open in the Excel window.

1 Introducing Office XP

Opening a File From Within the Windows Explorer

Another way to open a file is to double click the icon or the file name as they appear in the Windows Explorer. For example, double clicking the icon for the Access database file **Classic Cars.mdb** (page 19) starts the Access program with the **Classic Cars** file open. This method also works for other types of file such as Excel spreadsheets (**.xls**) and Word documents (**.doc**). In each case the program with which the file is associated is launched with the relevant file open on the screen.

Finding a File

When you save an important piece of work, note the folder in which the work is saved. If you've created a hierarchy of folders with meaningful names, this should help you to locate a file in future. There is also a search feature accessed off **Start**, **Search**, **For Files or Folders....**. Enter the file or folder name. If you don't know a file name, enter some text contained in the file itself. Then select the discs or folders to be searched and click **Search Now**.

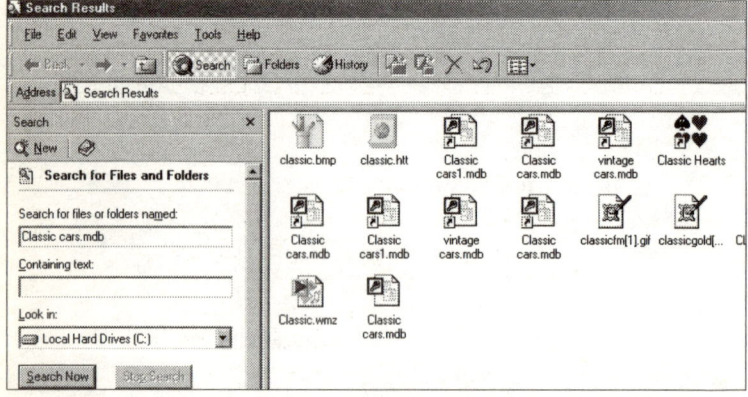

After the search is complete, files or folders matching the required description are listed. Double clicking an entry for a file in the list opens the file in its associated program, such as Word, Excel, Access or Paint.

2
Using Microsoft Word 2002

Introduction

Word 2002 is the word processing program supplied with the integrated software package Microsoft Office XP. There have been several editions of Microsoft Word, leading to this latest version, Word 2002. Currently Word is one of the most popular computer programs, widely used in offices throughout the world. The program contains lots of powerful features, enabling complex documents incorporating pictures and different styles of lettering to be produced. Even so, it's quite an easy program to use, working under the familiar Windows operating system found on most modern computers.

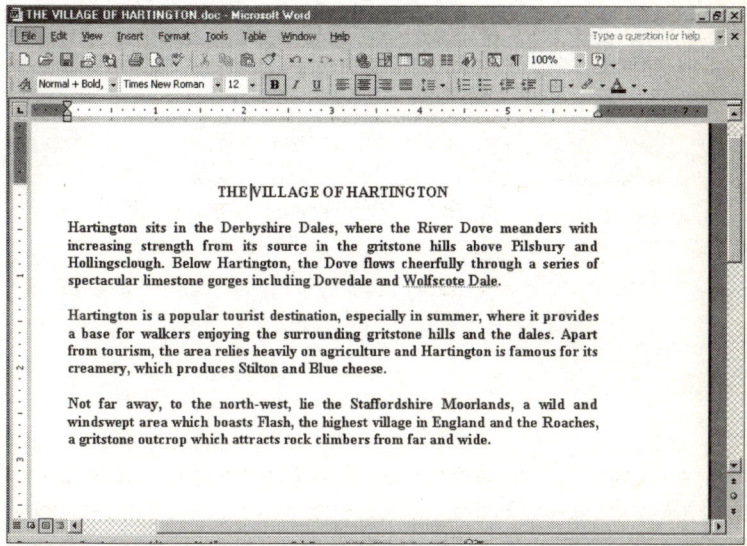

2 Using Microsoft Word 2002

Word Processing in Context

Word processing is one of the most frequently used computing applications in the office, the home and the small business. It's far more than a replacement for the typewriter as a means of entering text; modern word processors enable professional-looking documents to be produced easily, with very little specialist training.

Some of the advantages of the word processor, compared with the typewriter, are as follows:

- Corrections can be made on the screen before printing on paper, so there is no evidence of any alterations. Several copies can easily be printed.

- Documents are saved on disc, then retrieved later. This allows a document to be used again, perhaps with small changes such as a new date. This saves the time needed to retype the whole document.

- Text can be *edited* more easily – whole blocks of text can be inserted, deleted or moved to a new position in the document. The *Find and Replace* feature enables a word (or group of words) to be exchanged for another word or words, wherever they occur in a document.

- Text can be *formatted* in various fonts or styles of lettering and with effects such as bold and italic. The layout of the page can easily be changed, with different margins, line spacing, graphical effects and newspaper-style columns.

- Modern word processors contain many additional features such as spelling and grammar checkers, a thesaurus and a word count facility.

The ability to use programs like Microsoft Word 2002 is essential in the modern world, with increasing reliance on electronic communication, e-mail and the Internet.

Getting Started with Word 2002

This chapter is intended to show you how to do the most important basic operations with Word 2002. Each of the operations is described in detail, followed by an exercise to give practice in the skills just covered. If you have difficulty with any of the exercises, look back over the preceding notes to obtain the help you need. If you would rather use a keyboard than a mouse, a list of Keyboard Shortcuts is given near the end of the chapter.

The exercises in this chapter are similar to those used on the popular CLAIT course, from Oxford Cambridge and RSA Examinations. If you wish to assess your skills in relation to this course, a copy of the skills checklist is given at the end of this chapter.

The skills covered in the first section are as follows:

- Start up or *load* the Word program.
- Enter text.
- Save the text as a *file* on disc.

Starting the Program

The Word program is loaded by left clicking over **Start**, **Programs** and **Microsoft Word**.

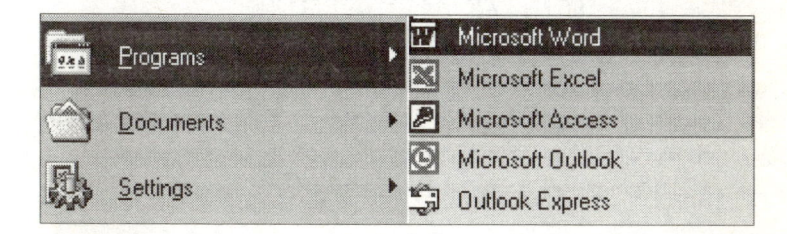

Alternatively, there may be a shortcut icon for Microsoft Word on the Windows desktop. In this case, double-click the icon to load the Word program.

2 Using Microsoft Word 2002

Features of the Word 2002 Screen

On starting the program, the word processor *window* opens ready for you to begin typing. Notice that Word starts with a number of predetermined or *default* settings. For example, the lettering is set in the Times New Roman font in size 12. (A *font* is a style of lettering). For the time being it's probably best to accept the default settings, although they can be altered later to suit your preferences.

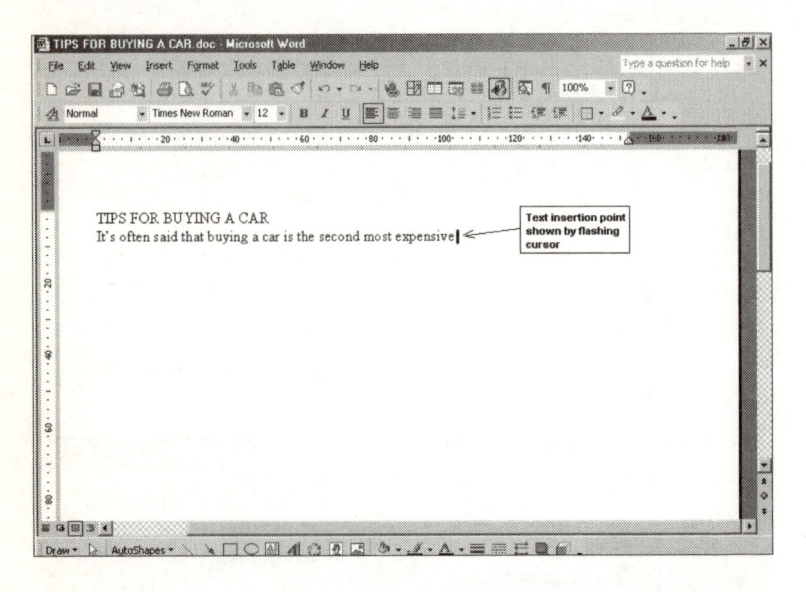

![Screenshot of Microsoft Word 2002 window showing a document titled "TIPS FOR BUYING A CAR.doc" with the text "TIPS FOR BUYING A CAR" and "It's often said that buying a car is the second most expensive" followed by a callout labeled "Text insertion point shown by flashing cursor"]

Across the top of the Word window is the *Title Bar*, which shows the name of the current document or piece of work, in this case **TIPS FOR BUYING A CAR.doc**. When you save a piece of text on disc, the computer automatically adds the extension **.doc** to the name of the file, to denote a Word document.

In the window shown above, the row beginning with the words **File**, **Edit**, **View**, etc., is the *Menu Bar*. Clicking any of the words reveals a drop-down menu of commands, to be selected with the mouse. As an example, the drop-down **File** menu is shown on the next page.

Using Microsoft Word 2002   2

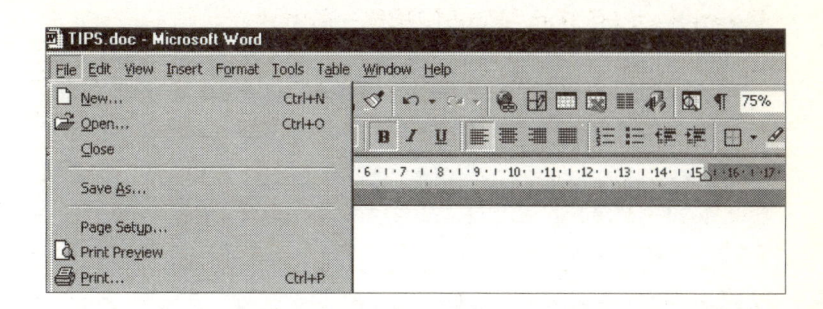

Under the Menu Bar is the *Standard Toolbar*, which consists of a row of small pictures or *icons,* as shown below.

Simply click on the appropriate icon to quickly carry out one of the common word processing tasks. For example, there are icons to save your work on disc and to print on paper.

    Save on disc   **Print on paper**

In general, you can reveal the function of any of the icons on the screen by allowing the mouse pointer to "hover" over the icon for a short time. For example, allow the mouse pointer to dwell over the first icon on the Standard Toolbar, a small white rectangle as shown on the right. A note appears to explain that this particular icon opens a **New Blank Document**.

Underneath the Standard Toolbar is the *Formatting Toolbar*, shown below.

The Formatting Toolbar allows you to change the style and size of lettering and to apply effects such as **B**old, *I*talic and Underline. These and other effects are discussed in more detail later in this book.

Using Microsoft Word 2002

The *Horizontal and Vertical Rulers* allow measurements to be made in relation to the text on the screen. In particular the Horizontal Ruler can be used for altering the left and right hand margins and for setting the *Tabulation* stops used in the vertical alignment of text.

A choice of measurement units is available, including inches, centimetres and millimetres and this is discussed later.

Other features of the Word window include the *Horizontal and Vertical Scroll Bars* which allow you to move through a document to view different parts. There is also a set of *View Icons* which enable the current document to be displayed in several different layouts.

View Icons　　　　　　　　　　　　　　**Horizontal Scroll Bar**

Entering Text

- Capital or *upper case* letters are obtained by holding down the **Shift** key while pressing the required letter key. Press the **Caps Lock** key to switch on capital letters continuously.

- When entering text, don't press the **Enter** (or **Return)** key on reaching the end of a line. Word processors use a feature known as *word wrap* to adjust the ending of one line and the starting of the next. You only need to press **Enter** when you wish to start a new paragraph or to insert one or more blank lines.

- It's normal practice to leave a space after a comma and a full stop.

- Don't worry if you make a mistake - these can easily be corrected using the editing keys, described later in this chapter. After entering the text, save it on disc as described shortly.

Using Microsoft Word 2002

The AutoCorrect Button

This is a new feature introduced with Word 2002. The **AutoCorrect Button** appears next to a correction which has been made automatically while you were typing. For example, suppose you were typing the sentence below and incorrectly entered "**teh**" instead of "**the**". The **AutoCorrect** feature would automatically change the text to "**the**". If you pass the cursor over the text, any word which has been automatically corrected is highlighted by a small blue rectangle. Allowing the cursor to hover over this rectangle displays the **AutoCorrect Button**, as shown below.

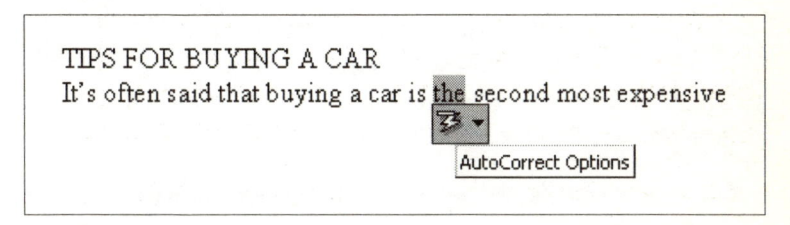

```
TIPS FOR BUYING A CAR
It's often said that buying a car is the second most expensive
                                      ⇗ ▾
                                      [AutoCorrect Options]
```

Clicking the down arrow on the right of the **AutoCorrect Button** (shown above) displays the **AutoCorrect Options** (shown below).

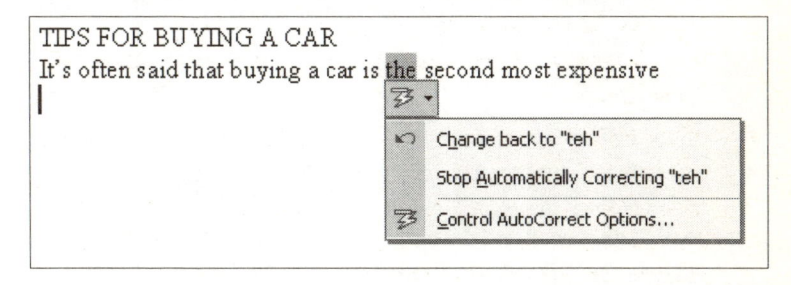

```
TIPS FOR BUYING A CAR
It's often said that buying a car is the second most expensive
                                      ⇗ ▾
|
                                  ↶  Change back to "teh"
                                      Stop Automatically Correcting "teh"
                                  ⇗  Control AutoCorrect Options...
```

The **AutoCorrect Options** enable you to "undo" the automatic correction, e.g. to revert to "**teh**" in the above example, if that's what you really intended. **Control AutoCorrect Options...** shown above, leads to the **AutoCorrect** dialogue box, which presents a full range of options. This dialogue box can also be accessed from the **Tools** menu and **AutoCorrect Options....**

Saving Your Work

To make a permanent copy of your work it must be saved on a disc. This usually means saving in a *folder* on the hard disc inside of the computer. Alternatively the work can be saved on a 3½ inch "floppy" disc if you need to transport it to another place.

Creating new folders of your own is described on page 19 of this book. For the time being however, it may be simpler to use the default folder **My Documents** which Windows provides for your work.

To save your work click **File** and **Save** from the Menu Bar or click the disc icon on the Standard Toolbar. The first time you try to save a new document the **Save As...** window opens showing the default folder **My Documents**.

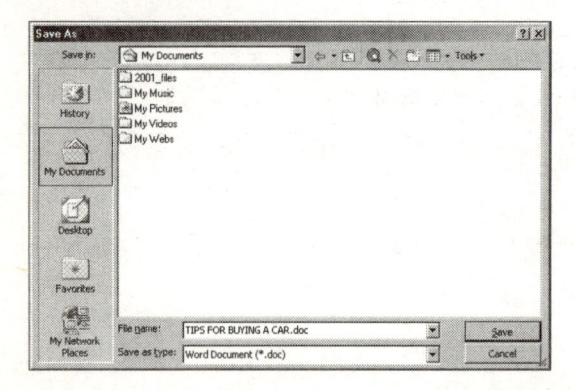

A piece of work saved on disc is known as a *file.* At the bottom of the **Save As** window you enter a **File name:**. The file name can extend to 255 characters and should ideally be *meaningful*, i.e. it tells you what the file is about. If you later modify your work and continue to save with the same file name, each new version will overwrite the previous one on the disc. To preserve each of the different versions of the work, save each time with a different name, for example **TIPS FOR BUYING A CAR 1** and then **TIPS FOR BUYING A CAR 2**, etc.

The AutoRecover Feature and Automatic Saving

If there is a power cut or your computer "crashes", you could lose a great deal of work. To avoid this, you can set Word to automatically save your work at regular intervals. This feature is set after selecting **Tools**, **Options...** and the **Save** tab. By default a file is saved every 10 minutes, but saving every 5 minutes will give greater protection.

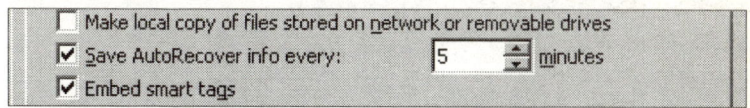

> ☐ Make local copy of files stored on network or removable drives
> ☑ Save AutoRecover info every: 5   minutes
> ☑ Embed smart tags

Even if you have switched on the **Save AutoRecover...** feature shown above, you should still carry out a full manual save when you finish work and at regular intervals in between. This is because the AutoRecover feature may not always succeed in retrieving all of a document.

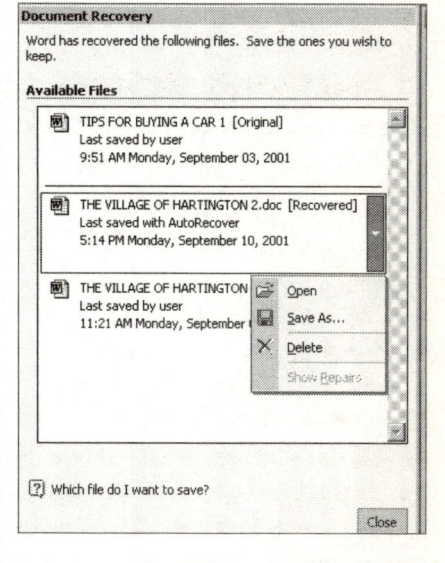

If disaster does strike and your work is interrupted by a power failure, when you restart the machine and launch Word, the **Document Recovery** task pane opens on the left-hand side of the Word screen. This lists the recovered files which were open at the time of the machine failure.

If the AutoRecover feature has saved a changed version of a file, this is listed with the note **[Recovered]** as shown right. Files which are unchanged since the last manual save are listed as **[Original]**.

When you pass the cursor over a recovered file listed in the **Document Recovery** task pane, a small down arrow appears on the right as shown above. Clicking the down arrow launches the drop-down menu shown above, with options to **Open**, **Save As...** or **Delete** the file.

2 Using Microsoft Word 2002

File Name Extensions

Notice that when a piece of work is saved, **Word 2002** automatically adds the file name extension **.doc**. Similarly, when a spreadsheet is saved in Microsoft Excel, the file name extension **.xls** is added. Microsoft Access database files are saved with the **.mdb** extension.

Saving Previously Saved Documents

Quick Save Using Existing Information

After you have saved a document for the first time, further saves can be done very quickly. Simply click the save icon on the Standard Toolbar or click **File** and **Save** off the Menu Bar. The file will be very quickly saved keeping the existing file name, save location and other information. *Previous versions of the file will be overwritten and therefore lost* during this type of quick save.

Saving With a Different File Name

If you want to save a file with a different name (in order to preserve previous versions), select **File** and **Save As...** from the Menu Bar. Then enter the new name in the **File name:** slot.

Changing the Save Location

To save the file on a different disc (such as a 3½ inch "floppy" disc) or in a different folder, select **File** and **Save As...** from the Menu Bar then click the down arrow to the right of the **Save in:** bar near the top of the **Save As** window. Select the disc on which to save the file, usually **Drive C:** or **D:** for an internal hard disc or **Drive A:** for a removable 3½ inch floppy disc. In the case of a hard disc with a hierarchy of folders, you will need to find and open up the folder in which you wish to save your work. This is done by double-clicking over the name or icon for the appropriate folder and sub-folders.

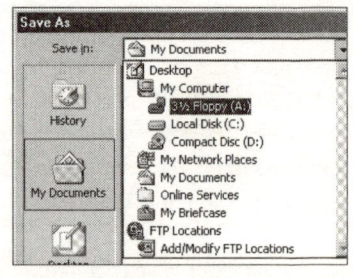

Exercise 1 - Entering and Saving Text

1. Load the Word program. Open a new blank page. Leave all of the settings at the default values.

2. Enter the following text as accurately as possible, inserting blank lines after the title and between paragraphs. Do not press **Enter** or **Return** at the end of a line of text but allow Word to use *word wrap*. (Do not use **bold** lettering, which is only used in the text below for illustration purposes).

TIPS FOR BUYING A CAR

It's often said that buying a car is the second most expensive purchase made by most people, after buying a house. Apart from the cost of the car, you must also budget for insurance, road tax and any repairs.

If you are under 25 years of age, the insurance is likely to be very expensive. Comprehensive insurance covers more eventualities than the cheaper alternative of Third Party, Fire and Theft.

When buying a second-hand car, great care must be taken to ensure that the vehicle is genuine. Ask to see any service records. Apart from showing whether or not the car has been regularly maintained, the records should also confirm the mileage. If you are not mechanically minded, arrange for a qualified motor engineer or experienced friend to carry out a thorough examination of the car. Some of the large motoring organisations provide an inspection service for prospective car buyers.

3. Check your work and correct any errors. Save your work on disc with a name such as **TIPS FOR BUYING A CAR 1**, in the folder **My Documents** as described on the previous pages. (If you save in a different folder, make a note of the location so that you can retrieve the file in future.)

4. Close down the word processor by clicking the cross in the top right hand corner of the Word 2002 window.

Editing Text

This section covers the following word processing skills:
- Load or open a previously saved document from disc.
- Edit the document to make changes and correct mistakes.
- Make a printout on paper.

Retrieving a File from Disc

After entering the text in Exercise 1, it should have been saved on disc as a file with a name such as **TIPS FOR BUYING A CAR 1**. To retrieve this text, look in the **New Document** task pane on the right of the screen, shown below. If the task pane is not visible click **View** and **Task Pane** form the menu bar then click the down arrow in the task pane and select **New Document**. To open a file from the task pane, click its name in the list of recently used files under **Open a document**.

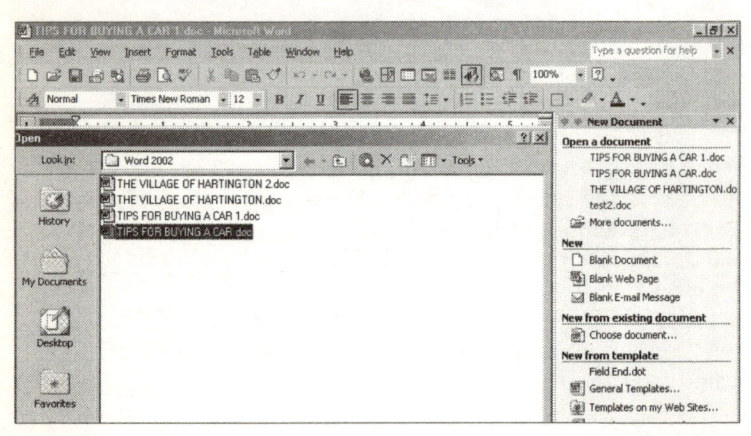

If the file doesn't appear in the list of recently used files under **Open a document**, select **More documents...** to launch the **Open** dialogue box, shown above. This will allow you to search your hard disc for the required file. Make sure the folder **My Documents** is selected. (If your work was saved in a different folder, use the **Look in:** bar to select the appropriate folder.) Now highlight the file name and click the **Open** button to display your work on the screen ready for editing.

Keys Used for Editing Text

If you are not very familiar with the keyboard, the following list gives the actions of some of the most important keys. These are used for *editing*, i.e. making changes to a document and correcting mistakes.

Moving About in a Document

There are several ways to move about a document. Many people find pointing and clicking with the mouse to be the simplest method. In larger documents you can drag the scroll box or click the scroll arrows. Skilled typists may prefer to use the four arrow keys shown right. The **Page Up** and **Page Down** keys allow you to scroll quickly through larger documents.

The **Home** key moves the flashing cursor to the beginning of a line of text. Pressing the **Ctrl** and **Home** keys together moves the cursor to the beginning of a *document*.

The **End** key moves the flashing cursor to the end of a line of text. Pressing the **Ctrl** and **End** keys together moves the cursor to the end of a *document*.

Inserting Text

To insert words in the middle of a sentence, place the cursor at the required insertion point and start typing. The new words should force their way in. If, however, the new words *replace* the existing words then *overtype mode* must have been switched on, in which case the letters **OVR** will appear on the *Status Bar* at the bottom of the Word screen. Simply switch overtype mode off by pressing the **Insert** key.

Deleting Text

Use the mouse or keyboard to place the flashing cursor on the left of the words or letters you wish to delete. Then press the **Delete** key to remove letters to the *right* of the cursor.

Letters to the *left* of the flashing cursor can be deleted using the **Backspace** key shown on the right.

2 Using Microsoft Word 2002

Block Operations

Sometimes it's convenient to carry out editing operations on highlighted *blocks* of text, rather than on individual words. A block of text may be just one sentence or it may extend to several pages. For example, you may wish to *delete* a whole paragraph of text or *move* it to another part of a document. The text must first be *selected* by highlighting it against a black background.

> It's often said that buying a car is the second most expensive purchase made by most people, after buying a house. Apart from the cost of the car, you must also budget for insurance, road tax and any repairs.
>
> If you are a young person under 25 years of age, the insurance is likely to be very expensive. The premium may also be higher if you live in an area where there is a greater risk of the car being stolen.
> Comprehensive insurance covers more eventualities than the cheaper alternative of Third Party, Fire and Theft.

Selecting Text Using the Mouse

- To select any piece of text, keep the left mouse button held down while moving the pointer across the whole of the required text.
- To select an individual word, double-click over the word.
- To select a line of text, make a single click in the left margin of the document.
- To select a paragraph, double-click in the left margin.
- To select the whole document, treble-click in the left margin or use **Edit** and **Select All** off the menus.

Selecting Text Using the Keyboard

You can also select the whole document using **Ctrl+A**. This means, while holding down the **Ctrl** (control) key, press the letter **A**. Another method is to place the cursor at the beginning of the required block of text then, while holding down the **Shift** key, (right), use the four arrow keys, as required, to select the block of text.

Using Microsoft Word 2002

Moving a Block of Text - Cut and Paste

When editing a piece of text, you may decide that a block of text should be moved to another part of the document. This is done on the computer using the *cut and paste* process, which imitates the physical operation using paper, scissors and glue.

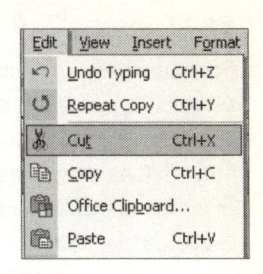

The steps in the cut and paste operation are as follows:

1 The block of text to be moved is selected, i.e. highlighted, as shown on the previous page.

2 The required block of text is *cut* using **Edit** and **Cut** from the menu shown above. Alternatively you can click the scissors icon on the Standard Toolbar. The cut operation removes the selected block of text from the document and places it on the *clipboard*, an area in the computer where text and graphics are temporarily stored.

3 The cursor is moved to the point where the block of text is to be inserted in its new position.

4 The block of text is *pasted* into its new position using **Edit** and **Paste** off the Menu Bar or by clicking the paste icon on the Standard Toolbar.

5 With the block of text in its new position, check that the spacing and punctuation around the block of text have not been altered during the move operation.

Copying a Block of Text

The method is similar to the cut and paste operation described above. The copy command is accessed from **Edit** and **Copy** from the menu shown above, or from its icon on the Standard Toolbar shown right. A *copy* of the block of text is placed on the clipboard then pasted into its new position, but the original block of text remains in its position in the document as before.

The Clipboard Task Pane

The clipboard is an area which stores pieces of text or graphics that you have cut or copied from one document prior to pasting into another document. Typically, a section of an Excel spreadsheet may be copied to the clipboard before being pasted into a Word document. Microsoft Office XP makes the clipboard and other features more accessible with the introduction of task panes on the side of the screen.

To make sure the task panes are displayed select **View** from the menu bar and ensure there is a tick next to **Task Pane**, as shown on the left. Now click the small down arrow on the top right of the current task pane (shown below left) to display the choice of alternative task panes. In this case, we need to select **Clipboard** to display all of the objects - pieces of text and graphics, etc. Alternatively select **Edit** and **Office Clipboard...** from the menu bar or double click the icon on the Windows Taskbar at the bottom right of the screen.

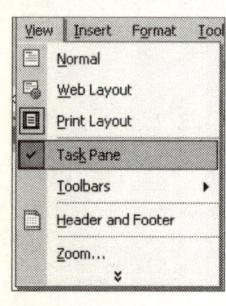

Text or graphical items which have been cut or copied appear on the clipboard task pane in miniature as "thumbnail" items. To paste an item into its new position, place the cursor at the insertion point in the document then click the item in the clipboard task pane.

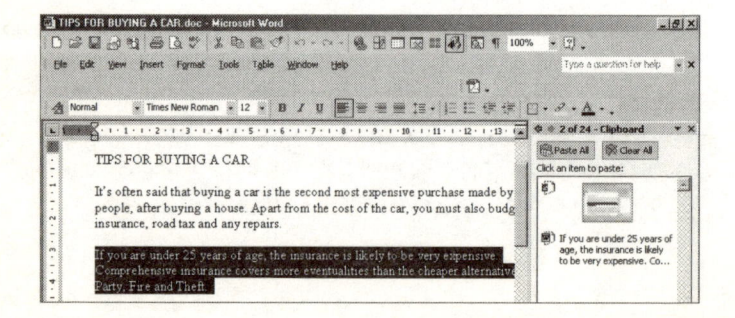

There are also options to paste or delete individual clipboard items or paste or clear all items on the clipboard.

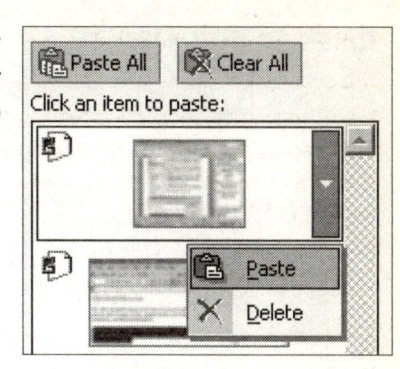

The Paste Options Button

If you cut a piece of text from a document and paste it into another position, a small icon appears near the new position of the text. This is the **Paste options button**, shown below.

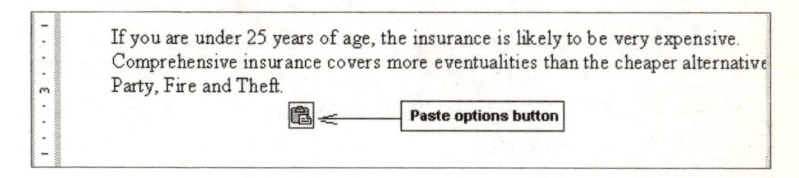

Allowing the cursor to hover over this button causes a small down arrow to appear. Clicking this arrow reveals a list of pasting options shown on the right. These give control of the format of the pasted text, e.g. whether to match the surrounding text in the new situation or to retain the format of the text in the original location.

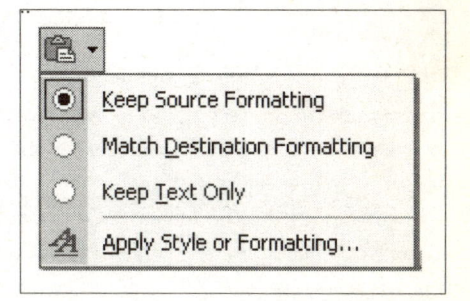

2   Using Microsoft Word 2002

Checking the Spelling

The spelling checker, accessed off **Tools** and **Spelling and Grammar...**, identifies spelling mistakes and suggests alternatives. Corrections are inserted using the **Change** button shown below.

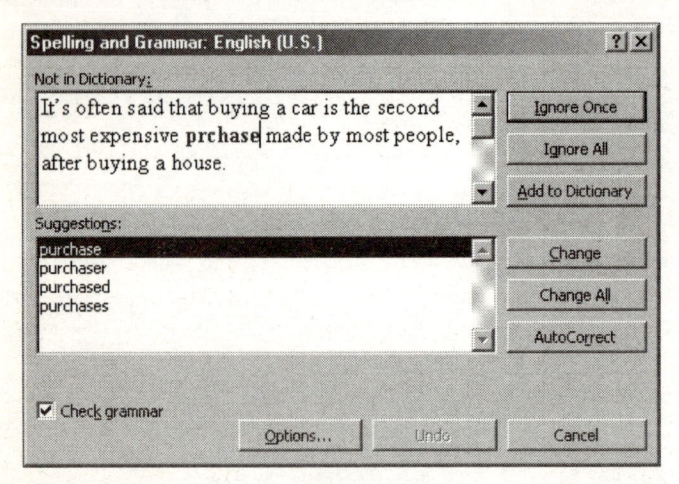

Not all mistakes are picked up. Where there are two correct spellings of basically the same word, for example, *principle* and *principal,* the program may not spot if the wrong version has been used in a particular context. As you are typing, words which are not in the Word 2002 dictionary are underlined, as if they are spelling mistakes. These words may in fact be correct, for example, unusual names of people or places.

If you make a simple error in a common word, such as "whihc" instead of "which", the program will correct the mistake automatically. This feature can be switched off by removing the tick next to **Check spelling as you type** accessed from the **Options...** button in the **Spelling and Grammar** dialogue box shown above. The **AutoCorrect** button, discussed earlier in this chapter, allows the user to undo the corrections, if necessary.

Please Note:

It's still essential to use careful traditional proof reading by eye, in addition to the computer spelling checker.

Using Microsoft Word 2002

Find and Replace

This feature is used to save time when you need to find all of the occurrences of a certain word (or group of words) and replace with another word or words. To open the **Find and Replace** dialogue box, click **Edit** and **Replace...** off the Menu Bar.

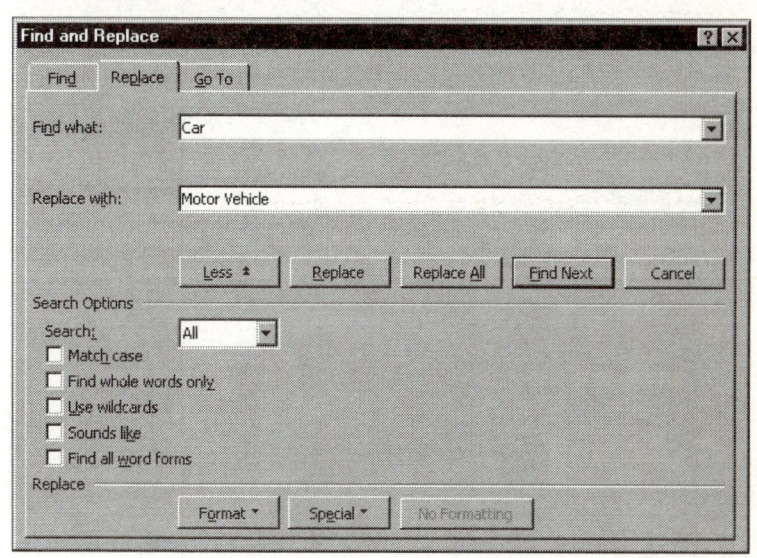

In the above example, the word **Car** is being replaced by the words **Motor Vehicle**. After entering the required words in **Find what:** and **Replace with:**, you have a choice. Click the **Replace** button to change the word(s) one at a time or click **Find Next** to move on to the next occurrence without making a replacement. Select **Replace All** to change all occurrences of the word(s) throughout the text.

A number of **Search Options** can be switched on using the check boxes at the bottom left of the **Find and Replace** dialogue box. For example, switching on **Find whole words only** would ensure that "Car " would be found but "Careful" would correctly be ignored. Similarly switching **Match Case** on in the above example would ensure that "Car" would be found but "car" would be ignored.

Printing Your Work

To make a printout of your work on paper, use **File** and **Print...** from the Menu Bar. This opens up the **Print** dialogue box shown below.

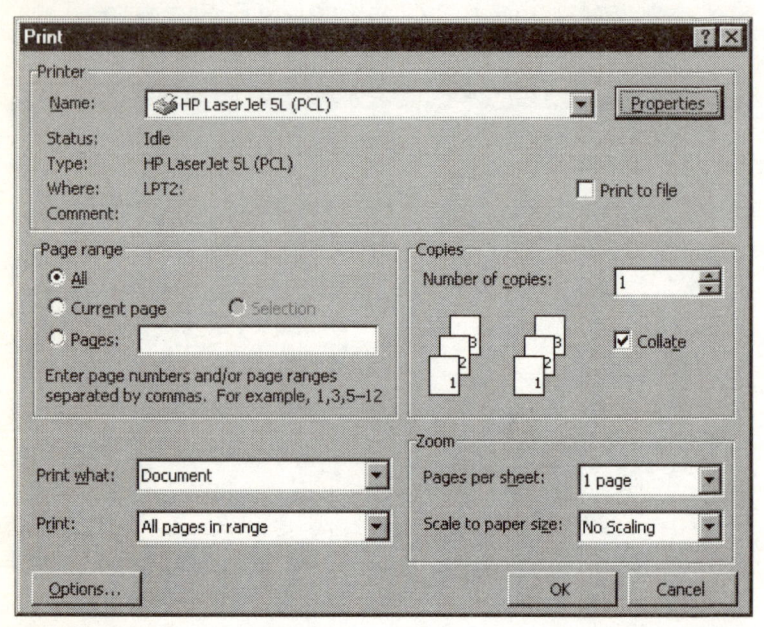

The **Print** dialogue box allows you to specify the number of copies and which pages are to be printed. Clicking the down arrow to the right of the **Name:** bar reveals a drop-down menu giving a choice of printers.

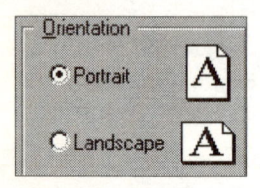

Click the **Properties** button and then specify details like the paper size and *orientation* - whether the page is to be printed in *portrait* format (long edge of the paper vertical) or *landscape* (long edge horizontal).

Printing Quickly

If you want to print quickly, bypassing the **Print** dialogue box and using the existing settings, click the printer icon on the Standard Toolbar, as shown on the right. (Or press **Ctrl+Shift +F12**).

Selecting **File** and **Print Preview** shows how a page will print on paper.

Exercise 2 - Editing and Printing

If you need any help with the skills in this exercise, please refer back to the notes on the previous pages.

If you prefer to use keyboard shortcuts rather than mouse activities, a list of the relevant key combinations is given on page 51.

1. Reload the file saved in Exercise 1, which you may have saved with the suggested name of **TIPS FOR BUYING A CAR 1**.

2. Carefully proof read the document and correct any mistakes using the methods described previously. Make a printout on paper.

3. Insert a new paragraph after ....**Third Party, Fire and Theft.** as follows:

    When you have been driving for several years without an accident, you should receive a No Claim Bonus, which entitles you to a discount on the insurance premium.

4. In the first paragraph, delete the sentence starting **Apart from the cost of the car...**.

5. Change the word **car** to **motor vehicle** throughout the document. (Make sure the **Find and Replace** option is set to **Find whole words only** as discussed in the previous notes.)

6. Move the second paragraph so that it becomes the third paragraph.

7. Save the file with a name such as:

    TIPS FOR BUYING A CAR 2.

8. Make a printout on paper.

2 Using Microsoft Word 2002

Changing the Format and Layout

This section shows how Word 2002 can be used to apply effects which change the format and layout of a document:

- Change the size of the margins
- Apply justification to the margins
- Embolden and centre text
- Change the line spacing

Changing the Page Margins

When you open a new page, the page will already be set up with default margins. These can be examined and changed if necessary by selecting **File** and **Page Setup...** from the Menu Bar.

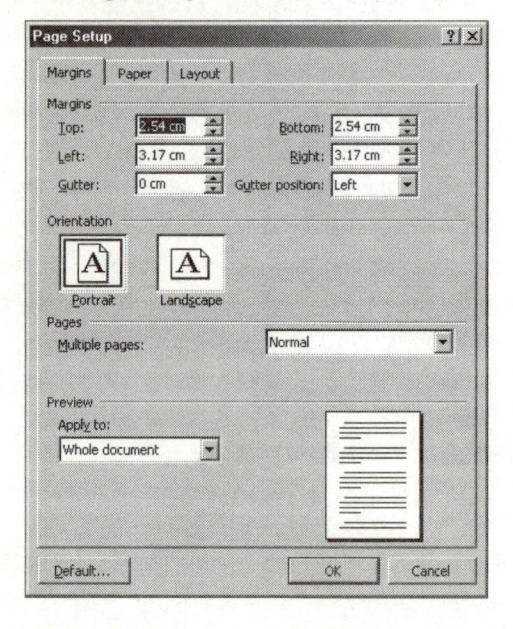

To change the **Left:** margin, for example, click one of the small arrows on the right to increase or decrease the margin from the default value of **3.17 cm**.

Indenting Paragraphs

The previous notes showed how to change the margins, which apply to the whole page. You can also *indent* a paragraph to make it stand out.

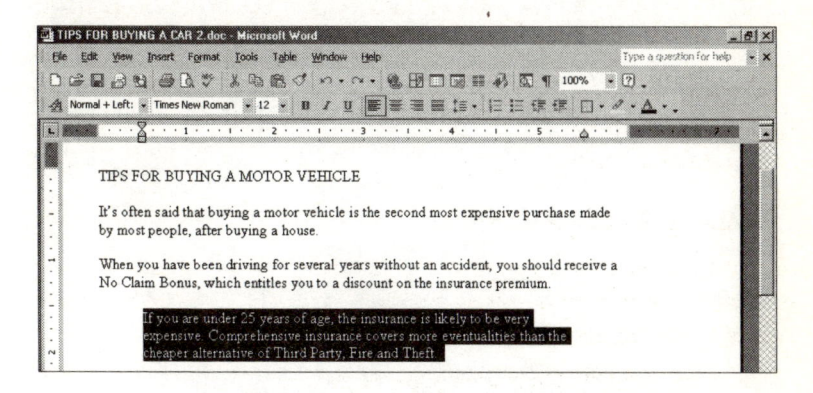

This can be achieved by selecting the required paragraph(s) as shown above. Then use the mouse to drag the lower *indent markers* on the left and right-hand side of the *Horizontal Ruler* as shown below.

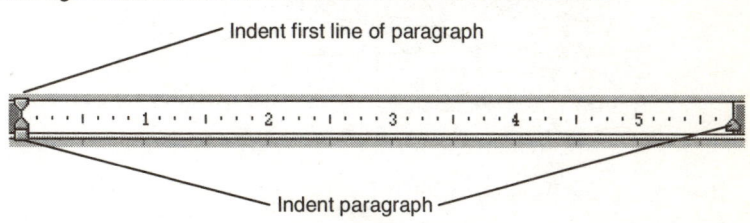

Indent first line of paragraph

Indent paragraph

The markers on the lower left and right-hand side of the ruler control the width of the whole paragraph. Note on the left-hand side of the ruler there are three markers. The upper marker controls only the indentation of the first line of the paragraph.

The middle marker produces a hanging indent where all but the first line of the paragraph is indented. Alternatively you can increase or decrease the indentation using the icons on the *Formatting Toolbar*, discussed earlier. Indents can also be set using the **Paragraph** dialogue box shown on the next page.

Changing Line Spacing

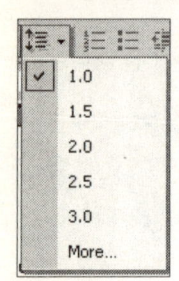

Sometimes you may want to set a paragraph or even a whole document with extra spacing between lines. Double spacing, for example, is often used on draft documents to allow space for amendments to be inserted manually. To adjust line spacing, first select the block of text to be changed. Then click the **Line Spacing** icon, shown right, on the formatting toolbar. Clicking the small down arrow on the right of the icon presents the choice of line spacing options shown above left.

Alternatively, after highlighting the block of text to be changed, select **Format** and **Paragraph...** and then the **Indents and Spacing** tab.

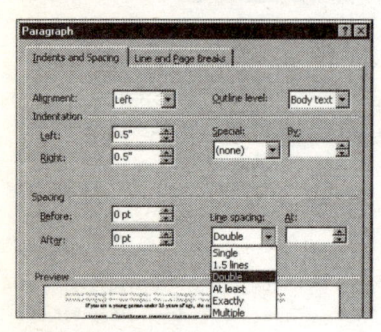

Click the down arrow under **Line spacing:** and select the required line spacing, before clicking **OK**. Line spacing can also be changed while typing within a paragraph. E.g. **Ctrl+2** gives double spacing. (**Ctrl+2** means "while holding down the **Ctrl** key, press the 2 key").

Changing the Measurement Units

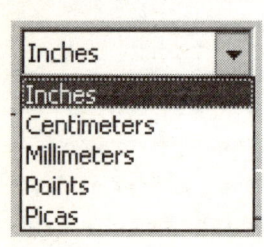

A choice of measurement units is available for the margins, indents and rulers, etc. The units can be changed after selecting **Tools** and **Options...** and the **General** tab. Click on the arrow to the right of **Measurement units:** to open the drop-down menu, then select the required units. Click **OK** to apply the new units.

Applying Formatting Effects:

Many of the formatting effects such as Bold, Italic and Underline and text alignment such as *centered* and *justified* can be applied using the same general method:

1. Select (highlight) the required block of text.
2. Apply the formatting by clicking the appropriate icon on the toolbar or by using the equivalent keyboard shortcut.
3. When the formatting has taken effect, remove the highlighting by clicking outside of the selected area.

The Formatting Toolbar

On the left is the font name and size, changed by clicking the arrows and selecting from the drop-down menus. Next come the three main text effects bold, italic and underline. These effects can also be switched on by holding down the **Ctrl** key and pressing either **B**, **I** or **U**. Effects like these operate as "toggles" - you use the same method to switch them on as to switch them off.

The next group of icons on the formatting toolbar represent different methods of text alignment. A straight vertical edge is known as *justified*. An irregular edge is known as *unjustified*. Reading from left to right, the actions of the 4 icons shown right and the alternative keyboard shortcuts are:

- Justified left edge, unjustified right   **Ctrl+L**
- Centered   **Ctrl+E**
- Justified right, unjustified left   **Ctrl+R**
- Fully justified text (justified left and right)   **Ctrl+J**
- Remove any of the above   **Ctrl+Q**

One problem with fully justified text is that in order to achieve the vertical alignment on the right-hand edge, the text may be filled with too many spaces between words producing unsightly "rivers of white".

Exercise 3 - Changing the Format and Layout

If you need help with any of the skills in this exercise, please refer back to the previous section. If you prefer to use keyboard shortcuts rather than mouse activities, a list of the relevant key combinations is given on page 51.

1. Load the file saved in Exercise 2, for which the suggested title was **TIPS FOR BUYING A CAR 2**.
2. Make a printout in single-line spacing and an unjustified right-hand margin.
3. Centre and embolden the title.
4. Set in the second paragraph by 1cm (or about ½ inch) at both left and right margins.
5. Save the file with a meaningful file name such as **TIPS FOR BUYING A CAR 3**.
6. Set the whole document in double-line spacing.
7. Set the right hand margin to justified.
8. Print the document.
9. Close the file and shut down the word processing system.

Keyboard Shortcuts

You may prefer to use the following keyboard shortcuts as an alternative to mouse operations. For example, to switch on bold lettering, use **Ctrl+B**. This means "While holding down the **Ctrl** key, press the **B** key."

Ctrl+C	Copy text
Ctrl+X	Cut text
Ctrl+V	Paste text
Ctrl+Z	Undo previous action
Ctrl+A	Select entire document
Ctrl+B	Bold text
Ctrl+U	Underline text
Ctrl+I	Italic text
Ctrl+E	Centre paragraph
Ctrl+J	Justify paragraph
Ctrl+L	Align paragraph left
Ctrl+R	Align paragraph right
Ctrl+Q	Remove paragraph formatting
Ctrl+1	Single-spaced text
Ctrl+5	1½ spaced text
Ctrl+2	Double-spaced text
Ctrl+N	Open new (blank) document
Ctrl+O	Open existing document
Ctrl+S	Save document
Ctrl+Shift +F12	Print document

In general, the above keyboard shortcuts are applied after first selecting the block of text. As described earlier, text is selected with the mouse or by holding down the shift key and traversing the text with one of the arrow keys. Please see **Block Operations** earlier in this chapter.

Effects such as Bold, Italic and Underline can be switched on before the text is typed. After typing the text with the effect applied, the effect is switched off by pressing the same key combination which switched it on. This "toggle" action is useful if you want to, say, highlight one or two words in bold or italic lettering in the middle of a sentence.

Exercise 4 - All Basic Word Processing Skills

This purpose of this exercise is to give practice in all of the word processing skills described earlier in this chapter. It's similar to a complete CLAIT assignment and covers all of the CLAIT word processing objectives.

1. Start up the computer and load the Word program.
2. Open a new document and enter the following text. (Do not use bold text)

THE VILLAGE OF HARTINGTON

Hartington sits in the Derbyshire Dales, where the River Dove meanders with increasing strength from its source in the gritstone hills above Pilsbury and Hollinsclough. Below Hartington, the Dove flows cheerfully through a series of spectacular limestone gorges including Dovedale and Wolfscote Dale.

Hartington is a popular tourist destination, especially in summer, where it provides a base for walkers enjoying the surrounding gritstone hills and the dales. Apart from tourism, the area relies heavily on agriculture and Hartington is famous for its creamery, which produces Stilton and Blue cheese.

Not far away, to the north-west, lie the Staffordshire Moorlands, a wild and windswept area which boasts Flash, the highest village in England and the Roaches, a gritstone outcrop which attracts rock climbers from far and wide.

3. Save the document as a file on disc.
4. Reload the file from disc.
5. Print a copy of the file, in single-line spacing and fully justified.

Continued

6   At the end of the first paragraph, after … **limestone gorges including Dovedale and Wolfscote Dale**… add the sentence **Unlike other villages of similar size, Hartington has a Town Hall and several Hotels and Public Houses.**

7   Delete the second sentence in the first paragraph … **Below Hartington, the Dove flows cheerfully through a series of spectacular limestone gorges including Dovedale and Wolfscote Dale.**

8   Move the second paragraph so that it becomes the third paragraph.

9   Replace the word **gritstone** with the word **rocky** wherever it occurs in the text.

10 Save the document as a file on disc and print a copy.

11 Centre and embolden the main heading.

12 Set in both right-hand and left-hand margins by 2cm.

13 Set the second paragraph in double-line spacing with an unjustified right-hand margin, with the remainder of the document in single-line spacing and justifed right margin.

14 Print a copy of the document.

15 Close down the system in the correct sequence making sure the data is secure.

If you have succesfully completed the above exercise then you may be ready to attempt one of the official CLAIT assignments from Oxford Cambridge and RSA Examinations.

You might also wish to assess your skills against the checklist provided on the next page.

Oxford Cambridge and RSA Examinations

Checklist of CLAIT Word Processing Skills

Objective		Achieved
1.1	**Enter and load text**	
1.1.1	Initialise application	☐
1.1.2	Enter text	☐
1.1.3	Load text	☐
1.2	**Edit text**	
1.2.1	Insert text	☐
1.2.2	Delete text	☐
1.2.3	Move text	☐
1.2.4	Replace words	☐
1.3	**Change the appearance of text**	
1.3.1	Change margins	☐
1.3.2	Alter line spacing	☐
1.3.3	Control justification	☐
1.3.4	Emphasise text	☐
1.3.5	Centre text	☐
1.4	**Save text, print text and exit application**	
1.4.1	Save text	☐
1.4.2	Print document	☐
1.4.3	Exit from application with data secure	☐

3

Using Microsoft Access 2002

Introduction

Microsoft Access 2002 is a leading database program, used to manage database files like the one shown below, displayed in *table format*.

MAKE	MODEL	COLOUR	PRICE £	REGISTRATION	DATE OF REG
MG	TD	BLUE	8500	TAF 21	12/03/59
AUSTIN HEALEY	SPRITE	RED	4900	MCH 459	01/08/65
PORSCHE	911	WHITE	14500	G826 FRA	04/06/91
LOTUS	ESPRIT	GREEN	11000	D213 GDP	20/03/86
AC	COBRA	BLUE	19900	DAX 423	04/05/92
PORSCHE	TURBO	RED	23900	PRS 525	03/04/77
MG	TF	RED	7500	FBL 319E	19/05/91
JAGUAR	E TYPE	WHITE	13500	LBC 191C	25/01/73
CHEVROLET	CORVETTE	YELLOW	7900	BAC 47	18/03/81
PORSCHE	928	BLACK	6000	ALE 923	21/11/83

The following definitions are used in the context of database files:

Record

A record is all of the information relating to one item such as a car or a person. In table format, one record is one *row* across the table. In the above table of 10 records, the fourth record is the **LOTUS ESPRIT**.

| LOTUS | ESPRIT | GREEN | 11000 | D213 GDP | 20/03/86 |

Field

When a database file is presented in the table format, a field is a vertical column, such as the **COLOUR** field shown in the above table. Each of the records above has 6 fields, with the *field names* **MAKE**, **MODEL**, **COLOUR, PRICE £, REGISTRATION** and **DATE OF REG**. In general, the data in a field may be *alphabetic*, (e.g.**ESPRIT)**, *alphanumeric* (e.g. **D213 GDP)** or *numeric* (e.g.11000). The way Microsoft Access 2002 handles these various data types is discussed later.

3   Using Microsoft Access 2002

File

A file is a collection of records, for example all of the cars in the London showroom of a nationwide dealer. Every record in the file has the same *record structure*, i.e. field names and data types. A database file is saved on disc with its own *file name*, in a similar way to saving a document produced in a word processor.

Database

A database is a collection of files. So for example, a large car dealer might create a database for the whole business, containing several files of cars, one file for each of the showrooms across the country. In the example below, the **Classic cars** database has separate files for the Birmingham, London and Manchester showrooms.

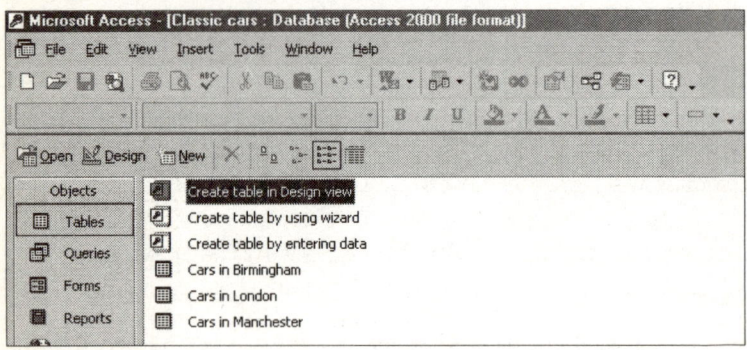

Note in the above database, the **Objects** column on the left lists different ways of organising the data, including the **Tables** layout already discussed. These are covered later, but briefly **Queries** presents the results of *searching* a file to find particular records or *sorting* into alphabetical or numerical order. **Forms** is an alternative to table format and shows the records on the screen one at a time, with the opportunity to include DTP features and graphics. **Reports** allow selected information to be extracted from a file and presented in a clear and stylish layout.

Designing the Record Structure

Before creating a file on the computer, we need to know the field names and data types for the records. This is the *record structure* and is identical for every record in the file. If you are designing your own file, it may help to sketch out the record structure on paper, as shown in the following example from the **Classic cars** database:

Field Name	Sample Data	Data Type
MAKE	CHEVROLET	Text
MODEL	CORVETTE	Text
COLOUR	YELLOW	Text
PRICE £	7900	Number
REGISTRATION	BAC 47	Text
DATE OF REG	18/03/81	Date

When you start creating the record structure on the computer, as discussed shortly, you can select the data type from a drop-down menu. In the above table, please note that the **Text** data type in Access will accept both letters of the alphabet and the digits 0-9. However, if a field will need sorting *numerically* then select **Number** as the data type.

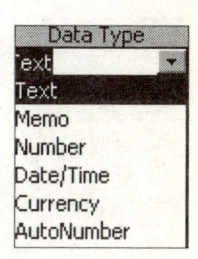

There is also a **Currency** format with several alternatives including £ signs and decimal places. However, since the **PRICE £** field above is entirely whole numbers this is left in the **Number** data type and **Long Integer** as discussed on page 61.

Access provides a choice of **Date** formats, and in this example **Short Date** is chosen for the **DATE OF REG** field.

3 Using Microsoft Access 2002

Creating a Database in Access

Microsoft Access is launched either from an icon on the Desktop as discussed in Chapter 1 or from **Start**, **Programs** and **Microsoft Access** as shown below.

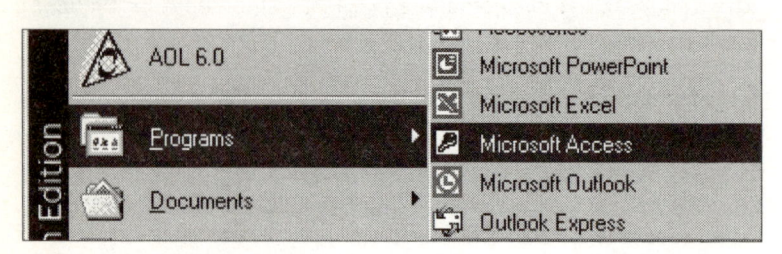

The Microsoft Access window opens showing the task pane on the right with options for creating a new database or opening an existing file. If the task pane is not visible, it can be displayed by selecting **View**, **Toolbars** and then **Task Pane**.

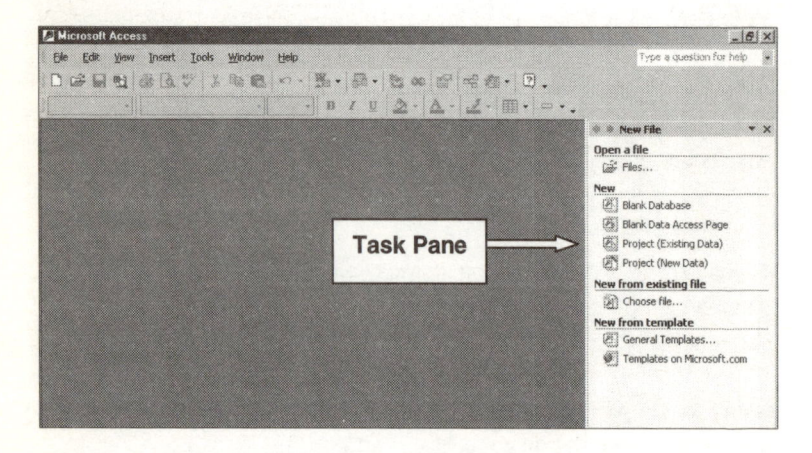

In this case, as we are creating a completely new database, select **Blank Database** under **New** in the task pane shown above.

Using Microsoft Access 2002 3

The **File New Database** window opens, allowing you to select, on your computer, the save location (folders or disc) for the new database. Click the down arrow to the right of the **Save in:** slot shown below and then select the required location. If necessary you can create a new folder after clicking the icon at the top right of the **File New Database** window as shown below.

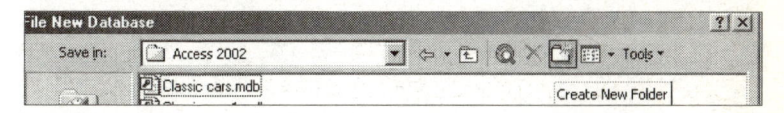

Now delete the default database name **db1.mdb** and enter you own name, such as **Classic cars** in this example. You don't need to type the extension .mdb - this will be added automatically.

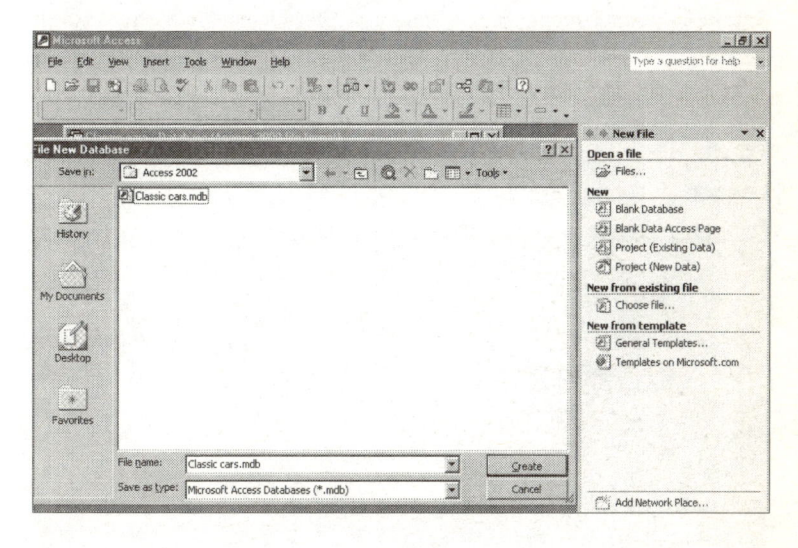

Please note that the name entered here represents a *database*, which is a container for a collection of files. Later on, individual files are created and saved within the database. In my example, the database is **Classic cars** and it will eventually contain separate files for **Cars in London**, **Cars in Birmingham**, and **Cars in Manchester**.

3 Using Microsoft Access 2002

Now click the **Create** button and you are given the choice shown below.

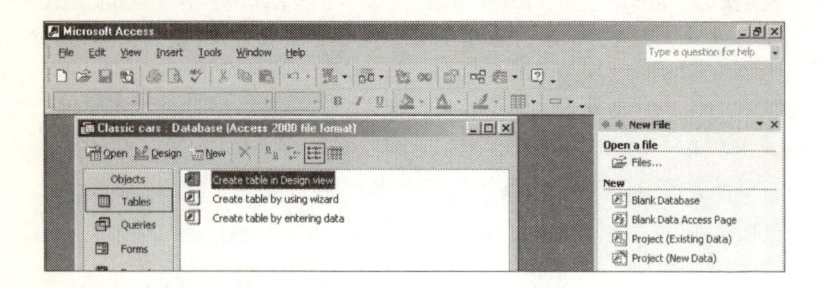

Select **Create table in Design view**, as this enables you to enter the field names and data types for the new file about to be created. Now click the **New** button and then select **Design View** and **OK** from the small menu which appears. Alternatively click the **Design** icon. The new database opens up in **Design View** showing a table ready for you to start entering the field names and data types. This table represents the first file in the database. Initially this is called **Table1** but later you will be able to supply a file name, such as **Cars in London** for example.

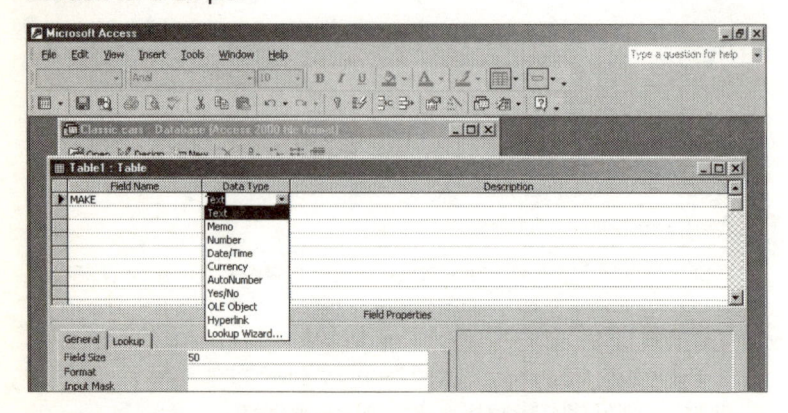

Continue entering the field names, pressing **Enter** or the arrow keys to move through the table. In the example shown, most of the fields can be set as **Text** as indicated on page 57.

Otherwise select the **Data Type** from the drop-down menu shown on page 60. Since the **Price £** field is whole numbers, i.e. integers, set **Data Type** as **Number**, **Field Size** as **Long Integer** and leave **Format** blank, as shown below.

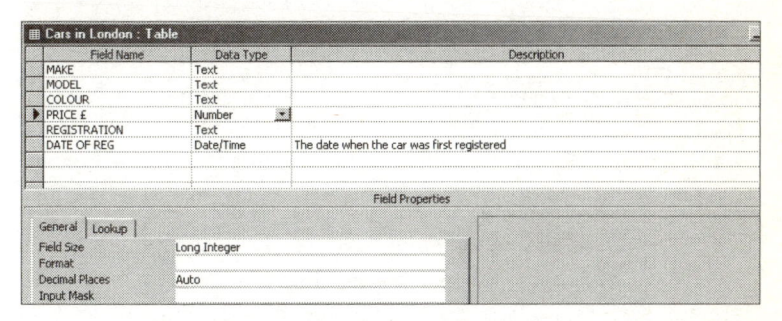

Field Name	Data Type	Description
MAKE	Text	
MODEL	Text	
COLOUR	Text	
▶ PRICE £	Number	
REGISTRATION	Text	
DATE OF REG	Date/Time	The date when the car was first registered

Field Properties

General | Lookup
Field Size — Long Integer
Format
Decimal Places — Auto
Input Mask

Similarly the **DATE OF REG** field is set to **Date/Time** for the **Data Type** and **Short Date** from the drop-down **Format** menu (shown on page 57). The complete record structure for the new file is shown below:

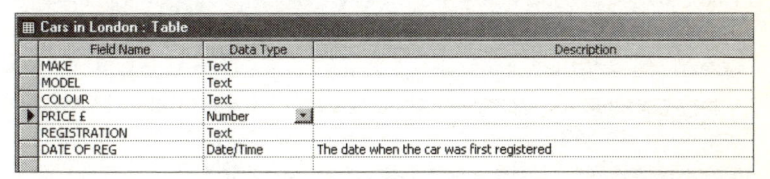

Field Name	Data Type	Description
MAKE	Text	
MODEL	Text	
COLOUR	Text	
▶ PRICE £	Number	
REGISTRATION	Text	
DATE OF REG	Date/Time	The date when the car was first registered

Entries in the **Description** column on the right are not compulsory, but allow you to add a fuller explanation of the field name if necessary.

Saving the Record Structure

When you have finished entering all of the field names, data types and any descriptions, you must save the record structure on disc. One method is to click **File** and **Save** off the Access menu bar. Alternatively, just click the **Close** cross in the corner of the **Design View** window. Access responds with the following message:

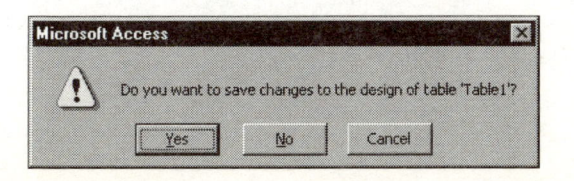

> **Microsoft Access**
>
> Do you want to save changes to the design of table 'Table1'?
>
> Yes | No | Cancel

3 Using Microsoft Access 2002

Click **Yes** and replace the default name **Table1** with a **Table Name** of your own such as **Cars in London**.

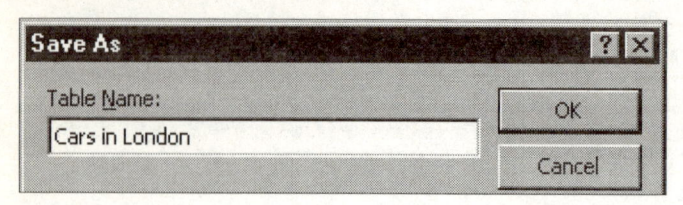

When you click **OK** you are confronted with what at first glance appears to be an error message.

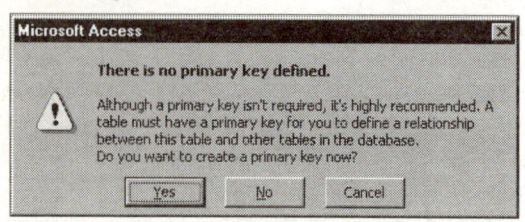

In fact it's simply a chance to give each record a unique identifier or **primary key** - useful in more complex databases. So if you click **Yes** the records will be numbered **1,2,3....** For the time being, however, simply ignore this opportunity and click **No**. You are returned to the database window showing an entry for the new file, **Cars in London**.

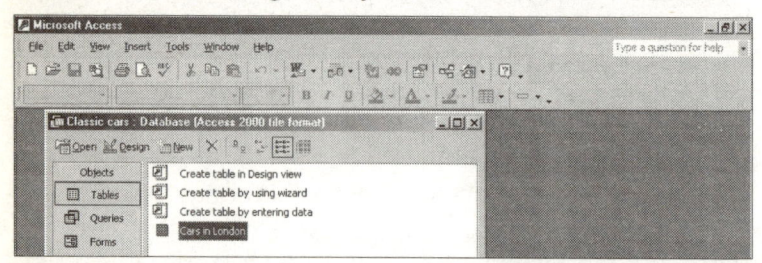

At this stage we have only set up a new database (**Classic cars**) and created the record structure for a new database file (**Cars in London**). We have yet to enter the actual *data* in the form of records for individual cars, such as **PORSCHE TURBO**, etc.

Editing the Record Structure in Design View

The record structure can be edited at any time, if you wish to change any field names or add or delete fields. Simply click the **Design** icon as shown left and you are returned to **Design View** as discussed on pages 60 and 61. Now you can make any alterations to the record structure such as changing a field name or data type.

Entering the Data

From the database window shown on the previous page, make sure the required table (**Cars in London**) is highlighted and click the **Open** icon. A blank table for the new file opens ready for you to start entering the records. This is known as **Datasheet View**.

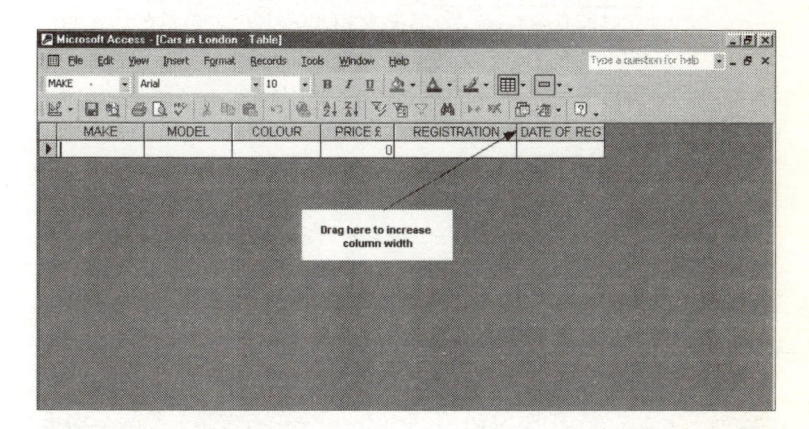

Altering the Column Width

The field names are already displayed across the top of the table and it's just a case of typing in the data in the rows below. In the above example, some of the columns were too narrow to display the complete field names. To alter the column width, move the mouse pointer onto the vertical line between the field names and wait until a cross appears. Then drag the cross to increase (or decrease) the width of the column.

3 Using Microsoft Access 2002

Entering the Records

Start typing in the records. You can move between fields using the **Enter** key, the arrow keys, the **Tab** key and the mouse. Don't worry if you make a mistake. You can always proof read the data then go back and make corrections later. Column widths may again need to be increased (as described on the previous page) if the data in the fields is too wide for the columns.

Saving a Table

The table can be saved by clicking the disc icon on the Access Toolbar. Alternatively, if you are ready to leave Datasheet View, clicking the **Close** cross at the top right of the Datasheet automatically saves the table.

Now the complete database file, **Cars in London**, including the field names (MAKE, MODEL, etc.) and the data (i.e. the car records), has been created and saved in table layout, as part of the **Classic cars** database.

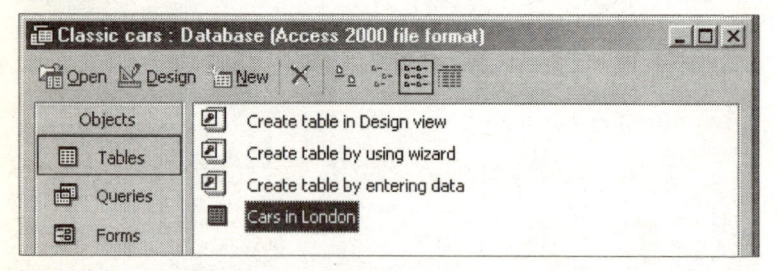

Opening a Saved Table for Editing or Finding Information

In future, to display the table **Cars in London**, either to *edit the data* or to look at the information in the records, highlight the table name, as shown above, and click **Open**.

To open the table to *edit the field names*, highlight the table name and click **Design**. The table opens in **Design View** showing the field names and data types ready for editing.

Exercise 5 – Creating a Database File

The following exercise covers essential skills for the general user of Microsoft Access 2002 and is also intended to provide practice for the student of CLAIT and IBT II.

Please refer to the previous notes if you need help with any of the skills in this exercise.

1. Start up the computer and load the Access program.
2. Open a new database with the suggested name **Classic cars**.
3. Create a new database file, in table format, using the following field names:

   MAKE
   MODEL
   COLOUR
   PRICE £
   REGISTRATION
   DATE OF REG

4. The **PRICE £** should be a numeric field. **DATE OF REG** should be set in the Date/Time data type (page 57).
5. Enter the data from the following table:

MAKE	MODEL	COLOUR	PRICE £	REGISTRATION	DATE OF REG
MG	TD	BLUE	8500	TAF 21	12/03/59
AUSTIN HEALEY	SPRITE	RED	4900	MCH 459	01/08/65
PORSCHE	911	WHITE	14500	G826 FRA	04/06/91
LOTUS	ESPRIT	GREEN	11000	D213 GDP	20/03/86
AC	COBRA	BLUE	19900	DAX 423	04/05/92
PORSCHE	TURBO	RED	23900	PRS 525	03/04/77
MG	TF	RED	7500	FBL 319E	19/05/91
JAGUAR	E TYPE	WHITE	13500	LBC 191C	25/01/73
CHEVROLET	CORVETTE	YELLOW	7900	BAC 47	18/03/81
PORSCHE	928	BLACK	6000	ALE 923	21/11/83

6. Save the table with a name such as **Cars in London**.

Editing the Data in a Previously Saved File

Having created a database file in table format, it will frequently need to be retrieved and opened for editing. For example, in a car showroom the price of a car may change, cars will be sold and new cars will be added to the stock. This will involve the following tasks:

- Altering the data in a field to reflect changes or to correct mistakes.
- Deleting records which are no longer required.
- Inserting new records.
- Saving and printing the modified file.

Start the computer and open up the Access program as described previously. Select **File and Open...** from the menu bar or **Open a File** from the task pane. Then locate your database within the folders accessed by clicking the down arrow to the right of the **Look in:** bar.

Highlight the name of the database and click **Open**. The **Classic cars** database opens showing an entry for the previously created table **Cars in London**.

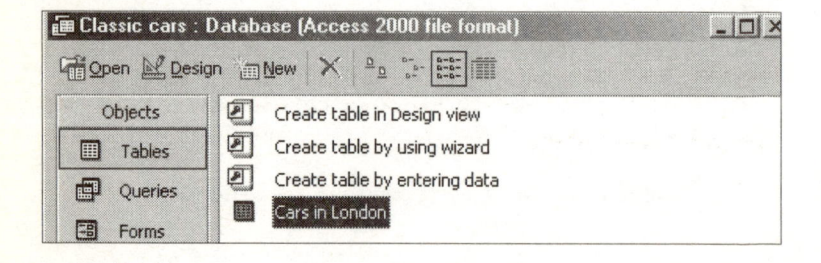

Make sure the required table, **Cars in London**, is highlighted and click the **Open** icon.

The **Cars in London** file opens in the table layout ready for editing.

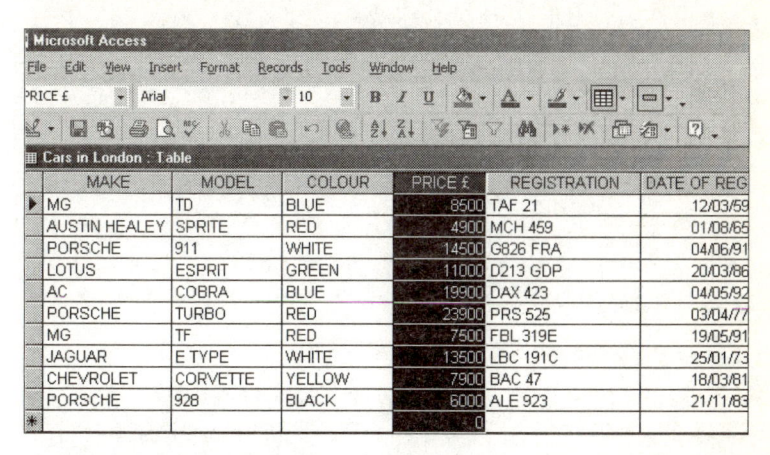

MAKE	MODEL	COLOUR	PRICE £	REGISTRATION	DATE OF REG
MG	TD	BLUE	8500	TAF 21	12/03/59
AUSTIN HEALEY	SPRITE	RED	4900	MCH 459	01/08/65
PORSCHE	911	WHITE	14500	G826 FRA	04/06/91
LOTUS	ESPRIT	GREEN	11000	D213 GDP	20/03/86
AC	COBRA	BLUE	19900	DAX 423	04/05/92
PORSCHE	TURBO	RED	23900	PRS 525	03/04/77
MG	TF	RED	7500	FBL 319E	19/05/91
JAGUAR	E TYPE	WHITE	13500	LBC 191C	25/01/73
CHEVROLET	CORVETTE	YELLOW	7900	BAC 47	18/03/81
PORSCHE	928	BLACK	6000	ALE 923	21/11/83
			0		

You can move about the table using the mouse, the arrow keys, the **Tab** key and the **Enter** key.

Recovering from Mistakes - Undo

If you make a mistake while editing, you *may*, if you're quick, recover the situation by clicking **Edit** and **Undo** on the Access Menu Bar or by clicking the **Undo** icon on the Access Toolbar.

To Edit the Data in a Field

Move to the required field and edit the data using the **Delete** and **Backspace** keys, etc., in the same way that text is deleted in a word processor. Then type in the amended data.

Deleting a Field (Column)

Highlight the entire vertical column representing the field, as shown above, by clicking the field name at the top of the column. Now select **Edit** and **Delete Column**.

3 Using Microsoft Access 2002

The following warning appears, informing you that both the field name and the data in the field are about to be permanently deleted.

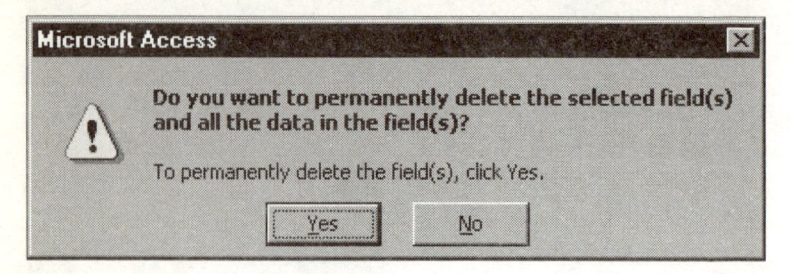

> **Microsoft Access**
>
> Do you want to permanently delete the selected field(s) and all the data in the field(s)?
>
> To permanently delete the field(s), click Yes.
>
> [Yes]   [No]

Inserting a New Field (Column)

Place the cursor in the column (field) to the right of the insertion position for the new column. Then click **Insert** and **Column** off the Access Menu Bar. A blank column, headed **Field1**, is inserted ready for you to enter the data for the new field, as shown in the table below.

MAKE	MODEL	COLOUR	Field1	PRICE £	REGISTRATION	DATE OF REG
MG	TD	BLUE		8500	TAF 21	12/03/59
AUSTIN HEALEY	SPRITE	RED		4900	MCH 459	01/08/65
PORSCHE	911	WHITE		14500	G826 FRA	04/06/91
LOTUS	ESPRIT	GREEN		11000	D213 GDP	20/03/86
AC	COBRA	BLUE		19900	DAX 423	04/05/92
PORSCHE	TURBO	RED		23900	PRS 525	03/04/77
MG	TF	RED		7500	FBL 319E	19/05/91
JAGUAR	E TYPE	WHITE		13500	LBC 191C	25/01/73
CHEVROLET	CORVETTE	YELLOW		7900	BAC 47	18/03/81
PORSCHE	928	BLACK		6000	ALE 923	21/11/83
				0		

Please note that a new column as shown above is automatically given the default field name "**Field1**". To change "**Field1**" to a more meaningful name, click the icon to switch to **Design View** and edit the field name of the new column. Click the icon on the Toolbar (shown left) to return to **Datasheet View** to continue editing the data.

Using Microsoft Access 2002

Deleting a Record

A record is one row across the table. Highlight the record by clicking in the square at the extreme left of the row. (If necessary, several records can be highlighted simultaneously by dragging the cursor).

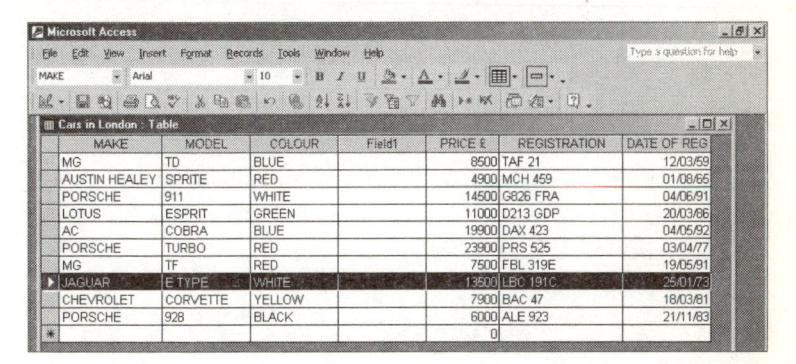

MAKE	MODEL	COLOUR	Field1	PRICE £	REGISTRATION	DATE OF REG
MG	TD	BLUE		8500	TAF 21	12/03/59
AUSTIN HEALEY	SPRITE	RED		4900	MCH 459	01/08/65
PORSCHE	911	WHITE		14500	G826 FRA	04/06/91
LOTUS	ESPRIT	GREEN		11000	D213 GDP	20/03/86
AC	COBRA	BLUE		19900	DAX 423	04/05/92
PORSCHE	TURBO	RED		23900	PRS 525	03/04/77
MG	TF	RED		7500	FBL 319E	19/05/91
JAGUAR	E TYPE	WHITE		13500	LBO 191C	25/01/73
CHEVROLET	CORVETTE	YELLOW		7900	BAC 47	18/03/81
PORSCHE	928	BLACK		6000	ALE 923	21/11/83
*				0		

The highlighted record(s) can be deleted by pressing the **Delete** key or by selecting **Edit** and **Delete** from the Access Menu Bar. The following message appears, warning that this operation cannot be undone.

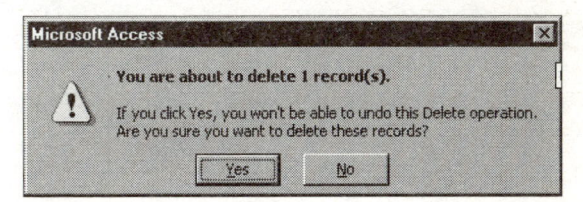

> **Microsoft Access**
>
> You are about to delete 1 record(s).
>
> If you click Yes, you won't be able to undo this Delete operation. Are you sure you want to delete these records?
>
> [Yes] [No]

Inserting a Record

From the Access Menu Bar select **Insert** and **New Record**. The cursor jumps to the next empty row at the end of the table, ready for you to enter the data for the new record.

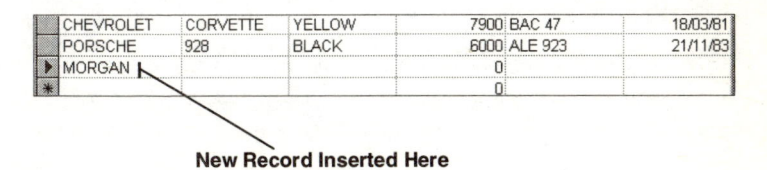

CHEVROLET	CORVETTE	YELLOW		7900	BAC 47	18/03/81
PORSCHE	928	BLACK		6000	ALE 923	21/11/83
▶ MORGAN				0		
*				0		

New Record Inserted Here

3 Using Microsoft Access 2002

Exercise 6 - Editing a Database File

The following exercise covers essential skills for the general user of Microsoft Access 2002. It is also intended as a practice exercise for the student of CLAIT and IBT II.

Please refer to the previous notes if you need help with any of the skills in this exercise.

1. Reload the database file created in Exercise 5, perhaps saved with the suggested name **Cars in London**.

2. Make a printout of the complete file on paper in table format. (Use **File** and **Print** off the Access Menu Bar or click the printer icon on the Toolbar.)

3. Make the following changes to the data:
   a) The **PORSCHE TURBO** should be **SILVER** not **RED**.
   b) The price of the **JAGUAR E TYPE** has increased to **£14,900**.

4. The **AC COBRA** has been sold. Delete all details of this car from the database file.

5. A new car has been acquired by the London showroom. The details are: **LOTUS ELAN, WHITE, £12,000** registration **RJG 239**, date of registration **23/09/73**. Add this record to the database file.

6. Save the database file.

7. Make a printout on paper in table format.

Recap

The previous pages have shown how to create a database file by saving the record structure and then entering and saving a set of records. Next the editing of the file was described, showing how the data could be amended to correct mistakes or to reflect new information.

The following section shows how the records in a file can be sorted into a particular order or searched to find records meeting specified criteria.

Retrieving Information

This section looks at the way a database file can be manipulated to provide specific information, as follows:

- Sort the records into alphabetical order.
- Sort the records into numerical order.
- Search the file to find records meeting a single criterion.
- Search the file to find records meeting multiple criteria.
- Save the database file and print only specified fields.

Queries - Sorting and Searching

Microsoft Access enables the sorting and searching of files to be carried out using a device known as a *query*. The end result of a query is a modified set of records in table format, resulting from the searching or sorting operations. This new table of selected or sorted records is referred to as a query and can be saved as a separate file with a unique name, for future reference. The query is designed using a grid into which you enter the sorting or searching criteria and the fields to be displayed in the resulting table.

Designing a Query

Start up the Access program and open an existing database such as **Classic cars** previously discussed. It will probably open with **Tables** selected in the **Objects** panel on the left-hand side. Click on **Queries** in the **Objects** panel to switch to the window shown below.

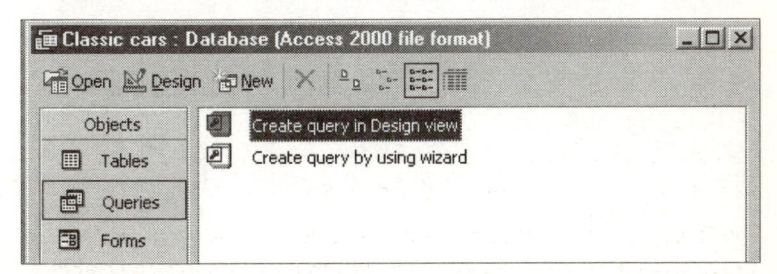

3 Using Microsoft Access 2002

Design   Make sure **Create query in Design view** is highlighted and click the **Design** icon. Or click the **New** icon and then select **Design View** from the resulting menu. This leads to a window showing the table(s) you have created in your database.

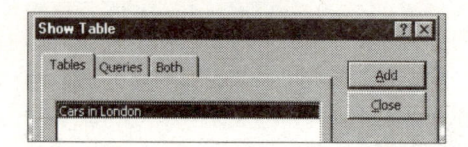

Highlight the table on which the query is to be based. In this example **Cars in London** is the only table available. Now click **Add** and **Close** to open up the query design grid shown below.

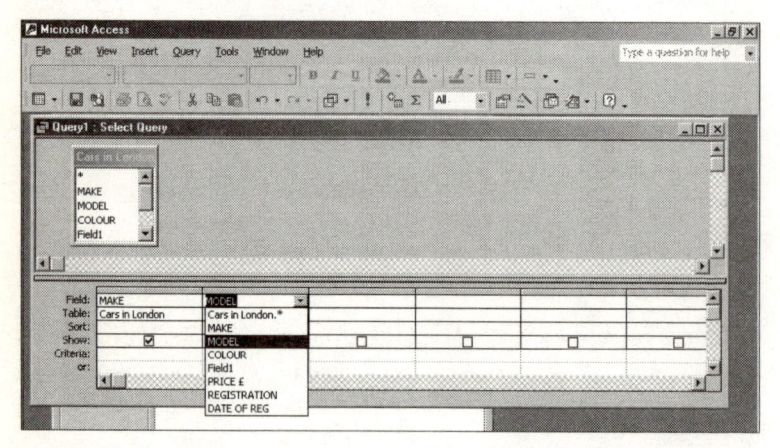

The query is built up in a number of stages. The initial setting up procedure is the same for all queries, which may be used for either *sorting* or *searching* the records. First, working along the row labelled **Field:**, click the down arrow in each slot to select a field you wish to display in the final query table. Also select the fields on which any sorting or searching operations are to be based. The selected field names should now appear along the row labelled **Field:** as shown on the next page.

Query - Sorting a File

Alphabetical Sorting

Suppose we want to sort the car file in alphabetical order of **MAKE** and then display only the fields **MAKE**, **MODEL**, **COLOUR** and **PRICE £**.

The query to achieve this is shown below.

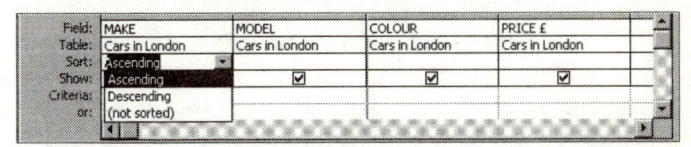

Field:	MAKE	MODEL	COLOUR	PRICE £
Table:	Cars in London	Cars in London	Cars in London	Cars in London
Sort:	Ascending			
Show:	Ascending	☑	☑	☑
Criteria:	Descending			
or:	(not sorted)			

Please note in the above query, **Ascending** or **Descending** order is selected by clicking the down arrow in the **Sort:** slot for the appropriate field, in this case **MAKE**. The **Show:** slot, when ticked, causes a particular field to be displayed in the query table produced by the sorting operation. If you don't want to display a particular field in the final sorted table, remove the tick in the **Show:** slot in the field.

Executing a Query

Having designed the query, it is executed by clicking the exclamation mark, shown right, on the Access Toolbar.

This produces the query table below, sorted in aphabetical order of **MAKE** and showing only the specified fields.

MAKE	MODEL	COLOUR	PRICE £
AC	COBRA	BLUE	19900
AUSTIN HEALEY	SPRITE	RED	4900
CHEVROLET	CORVETTE	YELLOW	7900
JAGUAR	E TYPE	WHITE	13500
LOTUS	ELAN	WHITE	12000
LOTUS	ESPRIT	GREEN	11000
MG	TF	RED	7500
MG	TD	BLUE	8500
PORSCHE	928	BLACK	6000

Numerical Sorting

In this example the table of cars will be sorted into numerical order of the **PRICE** field and only the fields **MAKE**, **MODEL**, **PRICE £** and **REGISTRATION** are to be displayed. The basic method is the same as for sorting in alphabetical order. From the database window, (page 71), make sure **Create query in Design view** is highlighted and click the **Design** icon. Or click the **New** icon and then select **Design View** from the resulting menu. Highlight the table on which the query is to be based (**Cars in London**) and then click **Add** and **Close** as described previously. The required fields **MAKE**, **MODEL**, **PRICE £** and **REGISTRATION** are selected after clicking the down arrows along the row labelled **Field:**. A sort in **Ascending** order is selected after clicking the arrow in the **Sort:** row of the **PRICE £** field, as shown below.

Field:	MAKE	MODEL	PRICE £	REGISTRATION
Table:	Cars in London	Cars in London	Cars in London	Cars in London
Sort:			Ascending ▼	
Show:	☑	☑	Ascending	☑
Criteria:			Descending	
or:			(not sorted)	

Now click the exclamation mark on the Access Toolbar to execute the sort. A table representing the car file sorted into numerical order of **PRICE £** is displayed. Only the fields specified in the query design (above) are displayed in the resulting table shown below.

MAKE	MODEL	PRICE £	REGISTRATION
AUSTIN HEALEY	SPRITE	4900	MCH 459
PORSCHE	928	6000	ALE 923
MG	TF	7500	FBL 319E
CHEVROLET	CORVETTE	7900	BAC 47
MG	TD	8500	TAF 21
LOTUS	ESPRIT	11000	D213 GDP
LOTUS	ELAN	12000	RJG 239
JAGUAR	E TYPE	13500	LBC 191C
PORSCHE	911	14500	G826 FRA
AC	COBRA	19900	DAX 423
PORSCHE	TURBO	23900	PRS 525

The Quick Sort

The Query method of sorting described on the previous pages produces a new, sorted table, saved as a separate query file. The previous unsorted table is preserved. However, if you don't need to keep a copy of the original unsorted table, you can carry out a *quick sort* as follows:

1 Open the required database table.
2 Select the field to be sorted by clicking in the field column.
3 Click one of the sort icons on the Access toolbar to select either ascending or descending order.

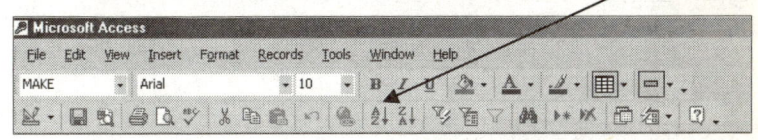

This method can also be used to sort on two or more *adjacent* fields. Simply highlight the fields to be sorted by dragging across the field names at the top of each column as shown below. Then click the icon for sorting in ascending or descending order as shown above. The records are sorted in order of their fields, starting with the left-hand column. In the example below, the records have been sorted first on the **MAKE** field and then on the **MODEL** field.

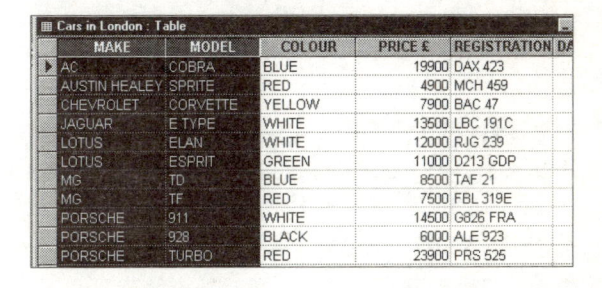

MAKE	MODEL	COLOUR	PRICE £	REGISTRATION
AC	COBRA	BLUE	19900	DAX 423
AUSTIN HEALEY	SPRITE	RED	4900	MCH 459
CHEVROLET	CORVETTE	YELLOW	7900	BAC 47
JAGUAR	E TYPE	WHITE	13500	LBC 191C
LOTUS	ELAN	WHITE	12000	RJG 239
LOTUS	ESPRIT	GREEN	11000	D213 GDP
MG	TD	BLUE	8500	TAF 21
MG	TF	RED	7500	FBL 319E
PORSCHE	911	WHITE	14500	G826 FRA
PORSCHE	928	BLACK	6000	ALE 923
PORSCHE	TURBO	RED	23900	PRS 525

Please note that for the CLAIT course it is better to sort using *queries* as described earlier, in which all unsorted and sorted versions of a table are saved as separate query files. These are needed for assessment purposes. The quick sort method described on this page does not keep the earlier versions of files.

Query - Searching a File

Searching involves scanning the file to find those records meeting certain *criteria*. Access carries out searches using queries, the result of a successful search being a reduced set of records saved as a query table.

Examples of Search Criteria

Single criterion: Find all **RED** cars in a file.

Multiple criteria: Find all **RED** cars, **PRICE** under £10000.

Sample Query

1   Search the **Cars in London** table to find all **RED** cars with a **PRICE** under £10000.

2   Display only **MAKE**, **MODEL**, **PRICE** and **REGISTRATION**.

From the database window, (page 71), make sure **Create query in Design view** is highlighted and click the **Design** icon. Or click the **New** icon and then select **Design View** from the resulting menu. Highlight the table on which the query is to be based (**Cars in London**) and then click **Add** and **Close** as described previously. The required fields **MAKE**, **MODEL**, **COLOUR**, **PRICE £** and **REGISTRATION** are selected after clicking the down arrows along the row labelled **Field:**.

Please note that although **COLOUR** is not required in the final table printed out, it is needed in the query design as one of the search criteria.

Entering the Search Criteria

In the **Criteria:** row enter **RED** for the **COLOUR**. (Always use the same *case*, i.e. capital letters in this example, and *exact spelling* as used in the actual data). Access automatically adds the speech marks.

In the **PRICE £** field enter **< 10000**. (< means "less than").

Field:	MAKE	MODEL	COLOUR	PRICE £	REGISTRATION
Table:	Cars in London	Cars in London	Cars in London	Cars in London	Cars in London
Sort:					
Show:	☑	☑	☐	☑	☑
Criteria:			"RED"	<10000	
or:					

In the row beginning **Show:** switch off the tick in the **COLOUR** field as this field is not required in the final table resulting from the query.

Now click the exclamation mark on the Access Toolbar to execute the search. A table showing any records matching the search criteria is displayed. Only the four fields specified in the query design are shown.

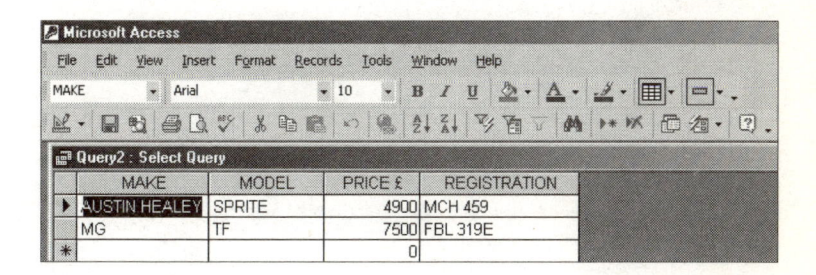

MAKE	MODEL	PRICE £	REGISTRATION
AUSTIN HEALEY	SPRITE	4900	MCH 459
MG	TF	7500	FBL 319E
		0	

Operators Used in Search Criteria

Microsoft Access uses the following operators for entering search criteria in queries:

< Less than   > Greater than

<= Less than or equal to   >= Greater than or equal to

The above operators may also be used to mean "alphabetically before" or "alphabetically after", etc.

E.g.

>="Simpson" means all names starting with Simpson to the end of the alphabet.

Saving a Query

Please note that a query is automatically given a working title such as **Query1**. However, you can save the query with a meaningful name of your own. This is done in **Datasheet View**, i.e. with the set of records produced by the query displayed on the screen in the table layout, as shown on the previous page. Click **File** and **Save** from the Access Menu Bar or click the cross to leave the query. The **Save As** box appears, enabling you to name and save the query.

After you have saved a query it is listed in the **Queries** window of the Access database as shown below.

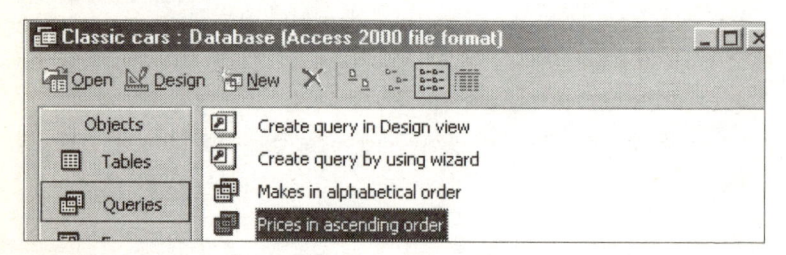

A query is a separate table of records created by sorting or searching the original file. From the window above, a **Query** can be opened at a later time for viewing or printing, by highlighting the query name and clicking the **Open** icon. An existing query can be modified after clicking the icon to enter **Design View**.

Printing a Query

Highlight the query name in the Access database window as shown above and click **Open** to display the table on the screen. To print the table select **File** and **Print** from the Menu Bar or click the printer icon shown on the left.

Exercise 7 - Manipulating a Database File

The following exercise covers essential skills in sorting and searching a database file. It is intended for the general user of Microsoft Access 2002 and also as practice for the student of CLAIT and IBT II.

Please refer to the previous notes if you need any help.

1. Reload the database file created in Exercise 6, perhaps saved with the suggested name **Cars in London**.
2. Sort the file into alphabetical order by **REGISTRATION**, save and print all the information in table format.
3. Sort the file into ascending numeric order by **PRICE** and print all the information in table format.
4. Search the file for all **RED** cars and print out all the information for the cars found.
5. Search the file for all **PORSCHE** cars costing more than **£10,000**. Print out only the selected records showing only the fields **MAKE**, **MODEL**, **COLOUR** and **PRICE £**.
6. Save the database file and close the Access program in the correct sequence with the data secure.

Recap

Exercise 7 completes the basic skills involving the creating, editing, sorting and searching of databases. On the next page there is a further practice exercise covering all of the database skills required for the CLAIT course. This is followed by a copy of the checklist of the CLAIT skills, provided by Oxford Cambridge RSA Examinations. You may wish to use this list in order to assess your personal progress.

The remainder of this chapter provides an overview of two further ways of presenting records, in addition to the table layout discussed so far. **Form View** displays records one at a time, with the ability to add graphic effects and insert pictures. **Report View** allows selected information to be printed in a polished and easy to understand style. Reports must be produced as part of the IBT II course.

3 Using Microsoft Access 2002

Exercise 8 - All Basic Database Skills

This exercise covers all of the basic database skills. It's similar to a complete CLAIT assignment and covers all of the CLAIT objectives.

This example involves a business dealing with holiday accommodation and you are required to set up a database of the available properties.

1. Start up your system and load the database application.
2. Create a database file using the following fields:

COUNTY	DESCRIPTION	HEATING
LOCATION	SLEEPS	PRICE £

3. Use the following codes in the **COUNTY** field:

COR	CORNWALL	YOR	YORKSHIRE
DEV	DEVON	PEM	PEMBROKESHIRE

   Enter the following data:

LOCATION	DESCRIPTION	SLEEPS	HEATING	PRICE £
CORNWALL				
NEWQUAY	BUNGALOW	4	ELECTRIC	299
MEVAGISSEY	COTTAGE	4	WOOD	339
WARLEGGAN	COTTAGE	5	OIL	369
ZENNOR	FARMHOUSE	6	GAS	499
DEVON				
COMBE MARTIN	COTTAGE	5	GAS	461
EXMOUTH	COTTAGE	4	GAS	405
MUSBURY	APARTMENT	2	OIL	345
YORKSHIRE				
INGLETON	COTTAGE	6	GAS	374
HAWORTH	COTTAGE	3	OIL	349
OAKWORTH	APARTMENT	2	ELECTRIC	290
PEMBROKESHIRE				
LAUGHARNE	BARN	2	GAS	265
PENDINE	FARMHOUSE	6	SOLID FUEL	484
LUDCHURCH	COTTAGE	2	GAS	269
STACKPOLE	FARMHOUSE	8	OPEN FIRES	494

4. Save your database and print all the data in table format.

5   A mistake has been made with the cottage at **HAWORTH**. It should be priced at **£359**. Please amend the record.

    The farmhouse at **STACKPOLE** now has **GAS** central heating. Please amend the record.

6   Delete the cottage at **WARLEGGAN** which is no longer available.

7   A new property is available in **DEVON**. It is an **APARTMENT** at **DARTMOUTH**, which sleeps **3**, with **ELECTRIC** heating and a **PRICE** of **£329** per week. Please add this record to the database.

8   Sort the file into ascending numerical order of **PRICE** and print all the data in table format.

9   Sort the data into alphabetical order of **LOCATION** and print all the data in table format.

10 Search for all properties costing less than **£300** per week and print out all the data for the records found.

11 Search the database for properties in **PEMBROKESHIRE** sleeping **6** or more people and print out the **LOCATION**, **DESCRIPTION** and **PRICE only** for these records.

12 Save your file and close the database application in the correct sequence with the data secure.

Oxford Cambridge and RSA Examinations

Checklist of CLAIT Database Skills

Objective	Achieved
2.1 Create a database structure and enter data	
2.1.1 Initialise application	☐
2.1.2 Create record structure	☐
2.1.3 Enter data	☐
2.2 Edit data	
2.2.1 Edit data	☐
2.2.2 Add a record	☐
2.2.3 Delete a record	☐
2.3 Manipulate data	
2.3.1 Sort records alphabetically	☐
2.3.2 Sort records numerically	☐
2.3.3 Select records specified by a single criterion	☐
2.3.4 Select records specified by more than one criterion	☐
2.3.5 Present specified fields from selected records	☐
2.4 Save a database, print contents and exit application	
2.4.1 Save data	☐
2.4.2 Print data	☐
2.4.3 Exit from application with data secure.	☐

Using Microsoft Access 2002 3

Form View

This is a different way of presenting records, as an alternative to the table layout previously discussed. Each record is displayed individually on the screen and can include various graphical styles and pictures.

This layout might allow, for example, a prospective house purchaser to study the full details of a house before scrolling on to the next.

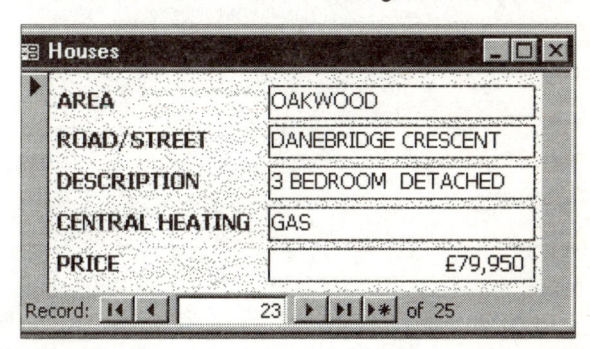

Creating a Form

With the database window open as shown below, select **Forms** from the **Objects** panel on the left-hand side.

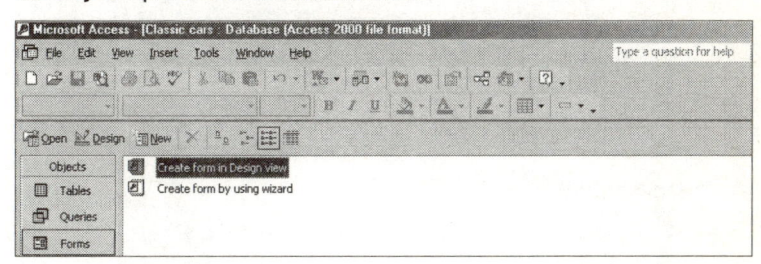

There is a choice either to **Create form in Design view** or **Create form by using wizard**. In this situation, the wizard provides a quick and easy way to achieve a professional result with very little effort. Form View takes its data from the records in a table or query which has already been created, as described earlier in this chapter.

3 Using Microsoft Access 2002

Creating a Form Using the Form Wizard

The **Form Wizard** allows a set of predetermined layouts and graphical styles to be used. From the database window select **Create form by using wizard**. From the **New Form** menu select **Form Wizard**.

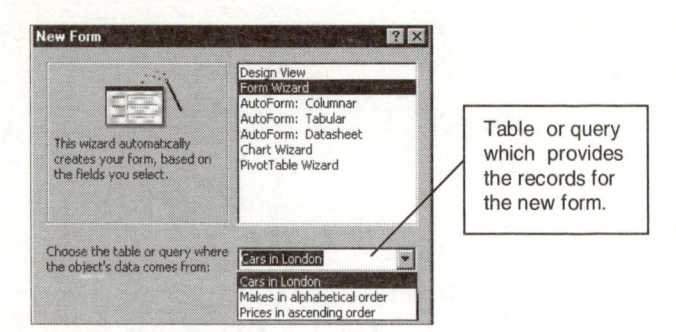

> Table or query which provides the records for the new form.

Now select, from the drop-down menu, the name of the table or query on which the form is to be based. Click **OK** and the **Form Wizard** presents a window for selecting the fields to be displayed on the form:

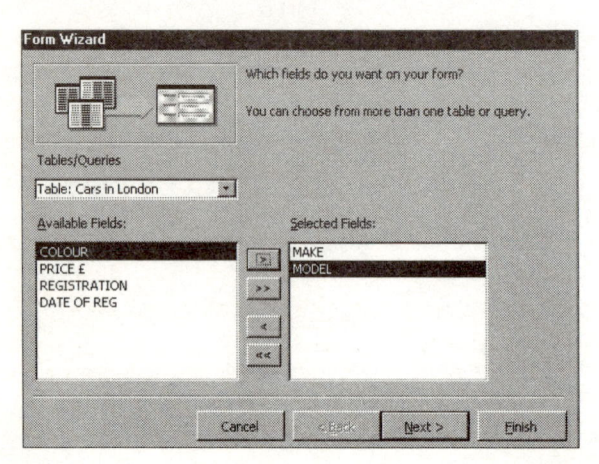

After selecting the required fields, click **Next** to move on to the next screen which allows you to choose the layout of the fields on the form.

Click **Next** again and you are confronted with a range of styles, giving a choice of various patterns of shading and different fonts.

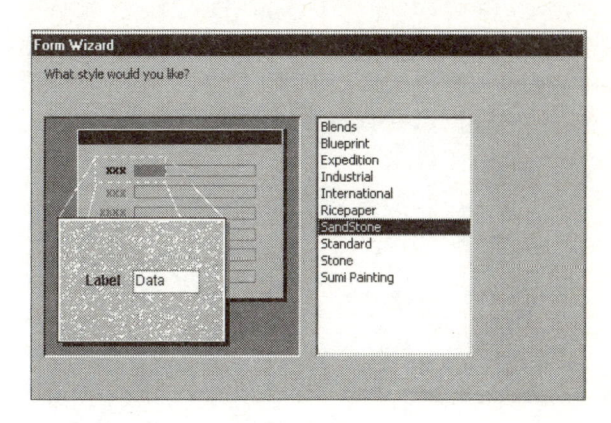

Add a new title, if necessary, then click **Finish** to see the new form.

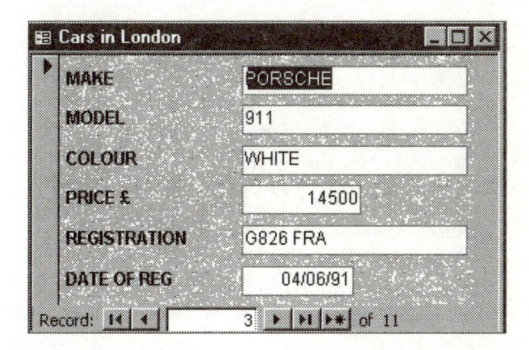

Move through the file of records in **Form View** by clicking the arrows.

If you want to create a form quickly, the form wizard reduces the task to one of simply clicking **Next** and selecting from menus. The form wizard in Access is very easy to use and provides a lot of built-in layouts and styles. In this situation the wizard is only altering the presentation of the data. The technical work is done when you create the original table on which the form is based.

3   Using Microsoft Access 2002

Creating a Form in Design View

If you highlight **Create form in Design view** (shown on page 83) and click **New**, the **New Form** window appears allowing you to select, from its drop-down menu, the table on which the form is to be based.

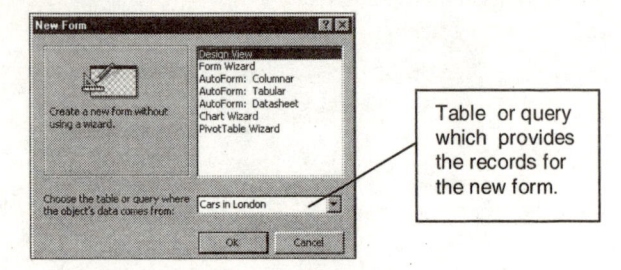

Table or query which provides the records for the new form.

Select the required table from the drop-down menu, in this example **Cars in London**. Highlight **Design View** and click **OK**. The **Design View** screen opens as shown below.

The field names are dragged from the list shown above and dropped onto the form, where they can be moved, if necessary, into their final position. A picture or piece of clip art can be inserted using **Insert** and **Picture...** off the Access menu. When the design is complete, click the cross to close **Design View** and save the form with its own name. Then when you open the form from the Access Database window, the data from the selected table or query will be inserted in the form layout.

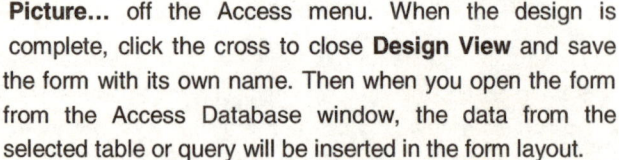

To edit the form design at any time in the future, click the **Design** icon on the Access Toolbar.

Reports

The **Report** feature in Microsoft Access allows a table or query to be presented in a style which is easy to read and understand. You can select which fields to include in the report. The report feature is part of the IBT II course and is ideal for making a stylish printout on paper, providing summarised information for reading away from the computer.

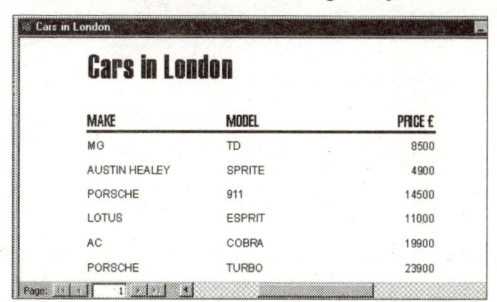

Creating a Report

The Report Wizard is very similar to the Form Wizard previously described. Like the form, the report takes its data from an existing table or query.

Start Microsoft Access and select the database to be used for the report. From the database window shown below, click **Reports** from the **Objects** panel and then select **Create report by using wizard**.

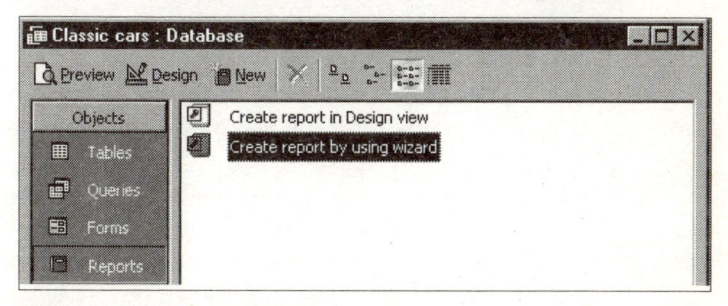

Click **New**, then from the **New Report** dialogue box which appears select **Report Wizard**. From the drop-down menu select the table or query on which the report is to be based.

Click **OK** and the wizard allows you to choose the fields to be included in the report.

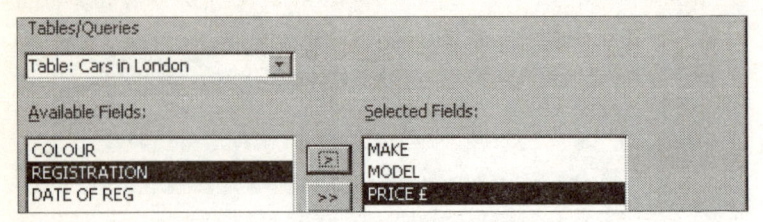

After choosing the fields and clicking **Next** there is an option to *group* the data in the report. Grouping on the **MAKE** field in a car file, for example, would place together the records of all cars by the same manufacturer. The records in the report can also be *sorted* on a selected field or fields.

The next dialogue boxes allow you to choose from various layouts and the orientation **Portrait** or **Landscape**.

Finally there is a choice of styles providing different fonts and graphics.

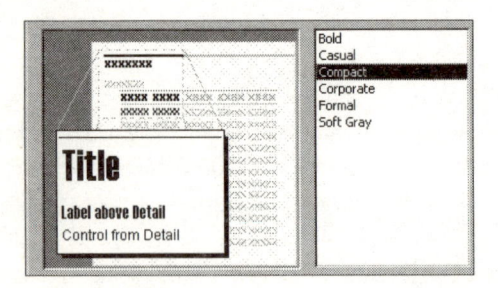

After clicking **Finish**, the report can previewed on the screen (as shown at the top of page 87) or printed on paper using **File** and **Print...**.

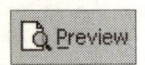

An existing report can be opened for viewing by highlighting the report's name in the Access database window and clicking the **Preview** icon.

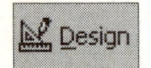

To edit the design of a report, highlight the report in the Access database window and click the **Design** icon.

4
Using Microsoft Excel 2002

Introduction

A spreadsheet is used for *calculations* in tables of figures. (If you only want to arrange data in neat rows and columns then it's more efficient to use the **Table** facility in a word processor such as Microsoft Word 2002.) A spreadsheet enables tables of figures to be easily displayed, calculated, sorted, printed and presented as graphs and charts.

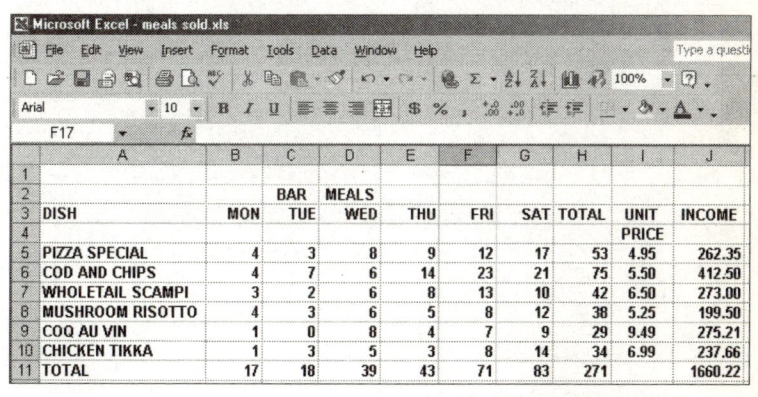

	A	B	C	D	E	F	G	H	I	J
1										
2			BAR	MEALS						
3	DISH	MON	TUE	WED	THU	FRI	SAT	TOTAL	UNIT	INCOME
4									PRICE	
5	PIZZA SPECIAL	4	3	8	9	12	17	53	4.95	262.35
6	COD AND CHIPS	4	7	6	14	23	21	75	5.50	412.50
7	WHOLETAIL SCAMPI	3	2	6	8	13	10	42	6.50	273.00
8	MUSHROOM RISOTTO	4	3	6	5	8	12	38	5.25	199.50
9	COQ AU VIN	1	0	8	4	7	9	29	9.49	275.21
10	CHICKEN TIKKA	1	3	5	3	8	14	34	6.99	237.66
11	TOTAL	17	18	39	43	71	83	271		1660.22

For anyone who doesn't like mathematics, the spreadsheet greatly simplifies and automates calculations - many complex mathematical tasks are reduced to entering numbers then clicking with the mouse.

Recalculation

Spreadsheet programs are widely used in business in a variety of applications. For example, you could enter the costs of the materials and labour and calculate the total cost of building a house. Then predict how possible alternatives affect the total cost of the house, such as:

"What if we used hardwood windows?"

"What if wages increase by 5%?"

4 Using Microsoft Excel 2002

To examine the effect of such changes on the total price of the house, you would simply enter the new costs in the appropriate part of the spreadsheet. The spreadsheet program would automatically repeat all of the calculations needed to arrive at the new total cost of the house. This *recalculation* feature is one of the main advantages of spreadsheet programs and can save many hours of work compared with traditional methods of calculation.

Microsoft Excel 2002 is also used for presenting data in the form of graphs and charts. This is covered in more detail in the next chapter.

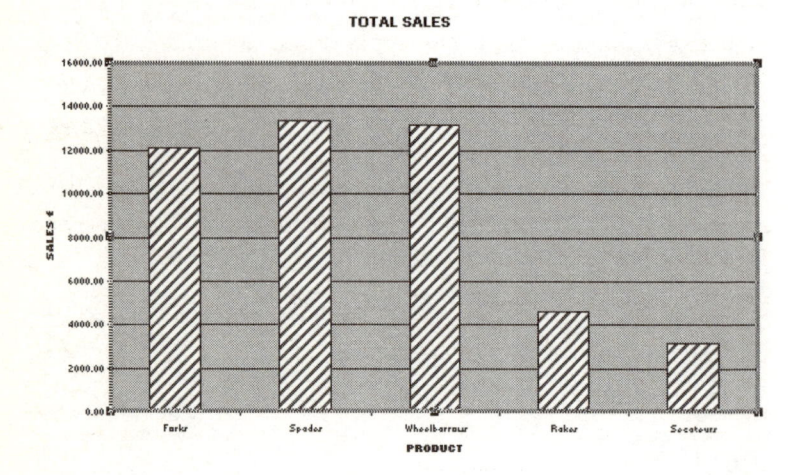

TOTAL SALES

The ability to use Microsoft Excel is an essential qualification for many jobs advertised in the national press. Spreadsheets are a major part of any Computer Literacy course, including the popular CLAIT scheme from Oxford Cambridge and RSA Examinations. For many of these courses, Microsoft Excel is the chosen spreadsheet software.

The remainder of this chapter describes the basic skills needed to create an Excel spreadsheet, including entering and editing the data, followed by methods of calculating, sorting and printing.

Getting Started with Excel 2002

The program is launched by clicking **Start**, **Programs** and **Microsoft Excel**.

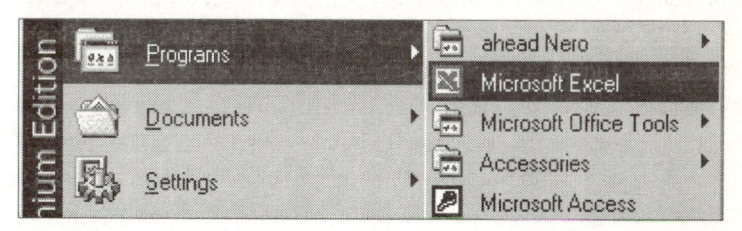

Alternatively, you may be able to double click a shortcut icon for Excel on the Windows Desktop - if such an icon has been created. Creating a shortcut icon for launching programs is described on page 13 of this book.

The Excel program starts by opening a new, blank spreadsheet as shown below. If the task pane is not visible on the right, select **View** and **Task Pane** from the Excel 2002 menu.

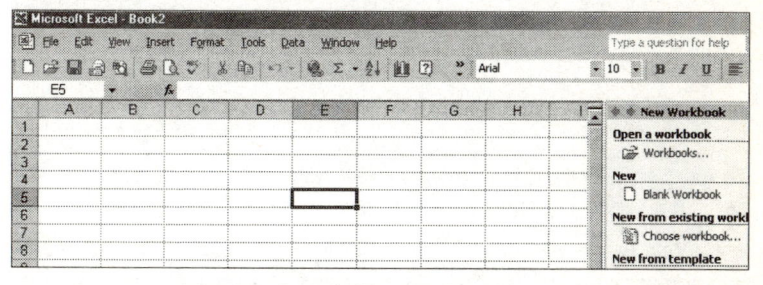

Across the top of the spreadsheet are the Menu Bar and Toolbar. The spreadsheet itself consists of a very large grid of small boxes known as *cells*, formed at the junctions of the vertical *columns* and horizontal *rows*. Each cell is uniquely identified by a "grid reference". In the above example, the rectangular cursor is highlighting cell **E5**. A practical business spreadsheet can be enormous, with thousands of rows and columns. This is made possible by extending the labelling of the columns beyond **A, B, C...** to include, for example, **AA, AB... GZ..., IS...**, etc.

Moving Around in a Spreadsheet

Using the Mouse

Move the cursor to the required cell and click to start entering text or data, etc. On large spreadsheets, drag the horizontal or vertical scroll bar to reach the required part of the worksheet.

Using the Keyboard

To quickly reach the beginning or end of a spreadsheet, use the key combinations **Ctrl+Home** or **Ctrl+End** respectively.

Scrolling can be achieved using the **Page Up** and **Page Down** keys.

When typing data in columns, the **Enter** key moves you down the column to the next cell.

The **Tab** key moves along a row from left to right.

Shift+Tab together moves along a row from right to left.

The four arrow keys allow the cursor to be moved around the worksheet in any direction.

Go To

To jump to a cell with a particular cell reference, select **Edit** and **Go To…**, then enter the **Reference**, e.g. **B5**, and click **OK**.

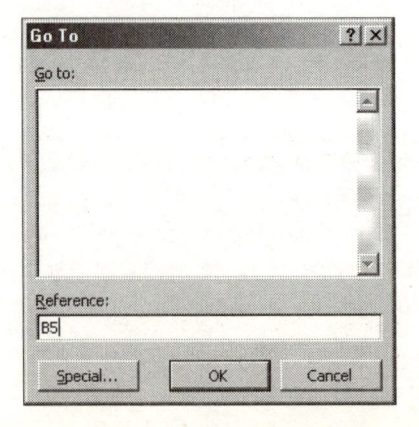

Cell Contents

Below the Toolbar is the Formula Bar, which displays information about the contents of the cell which is currently selected.

	A	B	C	D	E	F	G
1							
2			DRINK SALES				
3							
4		DESCRIPTION	PRICE	NUMBER SOLD	SALES		
5			£		£		
6		TEA	1.25	29	36.25		
7		COFFEE	1.29	35	45.15		
8		ORANGE	0.90	19	17.10		
9		LEMONADE	0.85	11	9.35		
10			TOTAL	94	107.85		
11							

Cell D10 contains the formula =D6+D7+D8+D9

Labels

From the above very simple spreadsheet, you can see that some cells contain words or *labels*, such as the title and the column and row headings, e.g. **DESCRIPTION**, **PRICE**, etc. To enter a label, simply click in the required cell and start typing. When you have finished typing, press **Enter** or use one of the other methods to move to the next cell. Labels can be edited at any time, after clicking in the appropriate cell.

Widening a Column

If a column is not wide enough for a label, place the cursor on the vertical line to the right of the letter at the top of the column. A small cross appears. This is used for adjusting the column width, as shown below.

Drag or double click the cross to alter the column width

Numbers

Click in the cell and type the numbers straight in. You can format the numbers later, e.g. to display every number with two decimal places or in *integer* format (no figures after the decimal point). Formatting numbers is discussed in more detail later in this chapter. If the numbers in the data are too wide for a cell, the screen displays ### instead of the numbers. To correct this problem, drag or double click at the top right edge of the affected column, as discussed on page 93.

	£
TEA	###
COFFEE	###

Formulae

A formula must be entered in the cell where the answer to a calculation is to appear. For simple tasks the formula can be typed in by hand.

All spreadsheet formulae start with the equals sign (=), for example:

=D6+D7+D8+D9 Add together the contents of cells **D6** to **D9**.

=D10-D8 Subtract the contents of cell **D8** from **D10**.

=C6*D6 Multiply contents of cell **C6** by contents of **D6**.

=E10/D10 Divide contents of cell **E10** by contents of **D10**.

Please note:

* is used as the spreadsheet multiplication sign.

/ is the sign for division.

While you are typing a formula, it is displayed both in the cell and in the **Formula Bar** near the top of the spreadsheet.

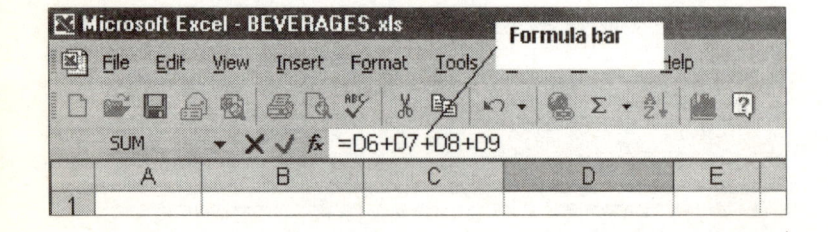

Using Microsoft Excel 2002

After you have finished typing a formula, press **Enter** or click the tick in the Formula Bar to complete the calculation. Now only the answer to the calculation appears in the cell - the formulae are not normally displayed in the cells.

Totalling Rows and Columns - the SUM Function

In the previous example, a column containing 4 numbers was totalled using the formula **=D6+D7+D8+D9**. In a more realistic spreadsheet it may be necessary to total hundreds of numbers down a column or along a row. For this task, Microsoft Excel provides the **SUM** function which can be typed by hand e.g.

=SUM(D6:D9)

In this example, **(D6:D9)** refers to the *range* of cells from **D6** to **D9** inclusive.

To save typing in by hand this frequently-used function, Excel provides the **AutoSum** icon on the Toolbar (shown left and below). If you select a cell then click the **AutoSum** icon, Excel uses its "intelligence" and assumes you want to add up the numbers above or to the left of the currently selected cell. The assumed range is shown dotted in the example on the left. This may or may not be the result you wish to achieve. Therefore you should always check that the range of cells which Excel has assumed is correct. If necessary, manually alter the range by editing in the cell or in the **Formula Bar** as shown below.

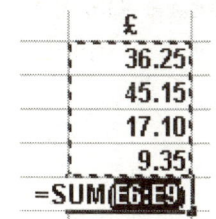

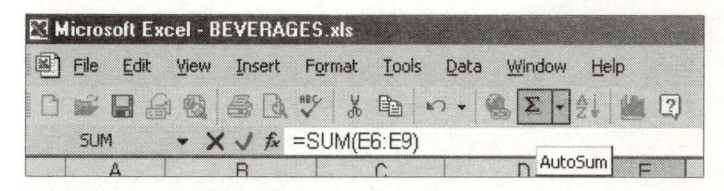

When you are satisfied the formula is correct either press **Enter** or click the tick in the Formula Bar as shown above, to complete the calculation. To redo the calculation from scratch, click the cross in the Formula Bar.

4 Using Microsoft Excel 2002

Editing a Cell at a Later Date

You can edit a cell containing a label, number or formula at any time in the future. The cell contents can be edited either in the cell or in the Formula Bar (sometimes also called the Entry Bar).

- To edit the cell contents by typing in the cell, *double click* in the cell and start editing.

- To edit the cell contents by typing in the Formula Bar, click once in the required cell then click in the Formula Bar and start editing.

Functions

For more complex calculations, a complete set of mathematical *functions* is available by clicking **Insert** from the Menu Bar then selecting **Function....** You can also access the functions by clicking the down arrow to the right of the **AutoSum** icon on the Excel toolbar.

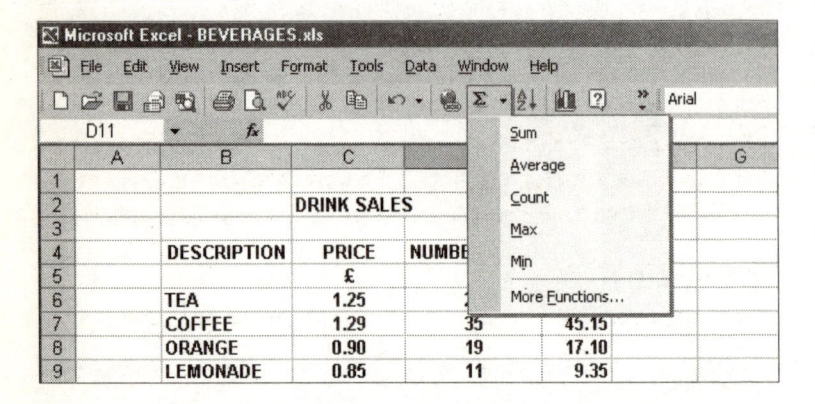

The more advanced mathematical functions are mainly used by technical specialists in applications such as science and engineering. General users, including students on CLAIT courses, will find the basic mathematical operations of addition, subtraction, multiplication and division more than adequate in most applications of spreadsheets.

Using Microsoft Excel 2002

Creating a Spreadsheet

This next section takes you through the following spreadsheet skills:

- Creating a spreadsheet
- Entering text and numbers
- Entering formulae, including replication
- Saving and printing the spreadsheet
- Printing formulae

The following pages describe the entry and calculation of the household spending spreadsheet shown below. You may wish to read through these notes then attempt the practical exercise on page 101. It is presented in the style of a CLAIT exercise.

Excel is loaded by clicking on the icon on the desktop or by selecting **Start**, **Programs** and **Microsoft Excel**. You are presented with a blank spreadsheet in which to start typing.

Entering Labels and Headings

Referring to the spreadsheet at the bottom of the page, first the title **HOUSEHOLD SPENDING** is entered. It may be helpful to keep the **Caps Lock** key switched on. Then the column and row headings can be entered. (Widening a column, if necessary, is described on page 93).

Entering Numbers

The numbers are typed straight into the cells. Formatting the numbers is dicussed later. It may be convenient to work down the columns, pressing **Enter** to move down to the next cell.

	A	B	C	D
1				
2			HOUSEHOLD SPENDING	
3	DESCRIPTION	JAN	FEB	MAR
4	FOOD	247.87	259.25	238.31
5	MORTGAGE	494.36	494.36	505.27
6	HEATING	86.32	79.48	69.99
7	ELECTRICITY	39.78	36.45	31.98
8	PETROL	159.82	198.72	121.49
9	ENTERTAINMENT	125.48	49.74	63.74
10	TOTAL			

4 Using Microsoft Excel 2002

Entering Formulae - Totalling a Column

A formula must be entered in cell **B10** to calculate the **TOTAL** expenditure in January.

	A	B
1		
2		HOUSEHOLD
3	DESCRIPTION	JAN
4	FOOD	247.87
5	MORTGAGE	494.36
6	HEATING	86.32
7	ELECTRICITY	39.78
8	PETROL	159.82
9	ENTERTAINMENT	125.48
10	TOTAL	=SUM(B4:B9)

To do this, click in cell **B10** then click the **AutoSum** icon off the Excel Toolbar. If you are happy that the range of cells within the dotted rectangle is correct, click the tick in the Formula Bar to carry out the calculation. Otherwise click the cross and type in the correct formula by hand.

When the calculation of the **TOTAL** is complete, the answer, not the formula is displayed in cell **B10**.

Replication

This is a great labour-saving feature of spreadsheets. Having calculated the total for January, the same method can be applied to February and March by a simple mouse operation.

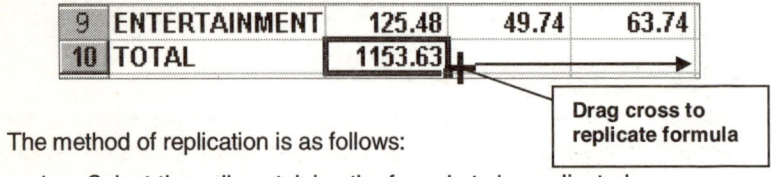

9	ENTERTAINMENT	125.48	49.74	63.74
10	TOTAL	1153.63		

Drag cross to replicate formula

The method of replication is as follows:

1. Select the cell containing the formula to be replicated.

2. Allow the cursor to hover over the bottom right-hand corner of the cell (the **Drag handle**) until a small cross appears.

3. Hold down the left mouse button and drag the cross over the cells where the calculation is to be replicated. The totals for February and March should appear in the cells automatically.

Please also see the notes on Auto Fill Options on pages 104 and 105 of this book.

Saving a Spreadsheet File

The spreadsheet is saved using **File** and **Save As...**, with a file name such as **household1**. Note that a spreadsheet is saved in the same way as a wordprocessing or database file, except for the **.xls** file name extension. (There is no need to type the **.xls** extension).

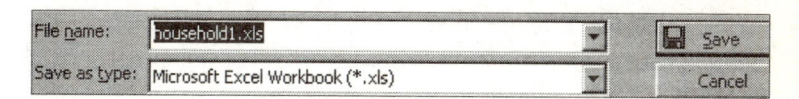

File name:	household1.xls
Save as type:	Microsoft Excel Workbook (*.xls)

Printing a Spreadsheet

An Excel spreadsheet is printed using **File** and **Print** from the menu. (A quick print using default settings can be carried out by clicking the printer icon on the Excel Toolbar.)

Gridlines

To print the horizontal and vertical gridlines select **File**, **Page Setup**, **Sheet** and switch on **Gridlines** under the **Print** heading.

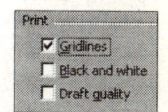

To display or switch off gridlines on the screen select **Tools**, **Options** and **View**. Then click the tick box to switch the **Gridlines** on or off.

Displaying and Printing Formulae

Calculated cells normally display the answers to the calculation, not the formulae themselves. When a calculated cell is selected by a single click with the mouse, the formula is displayed in the Formula Bar at the top of the spreadsheet. You can display a formula in an individual cell by double clicking in the cell.

To display all of the spreadsheet formulae in their cells select **Tools**, **Options** and **View** and make sure that the **Formulas** tick box under **Window options** is switched on as shown right.

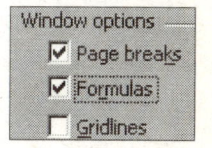

4 Using Microsoft Excel 2002

The household spending spreadsheet is shown below, with the option to display the formulae switched on.

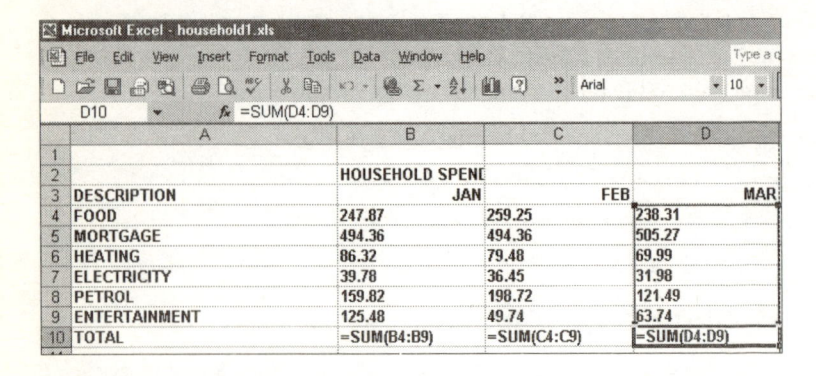

	A	B	C	D
1				
2		HOUSEHOLD SPEND		
3	DESCRIPTION	JAN	FEB	MAR
4	FOOD	247.87	259.25	238.31
5	MORTGAGE	494.36	494.36	505.27
6	HEATING	86.32	79.48	69.99
7	ELECTRICITY	39.78	36.45	31.98
8	PETROL	159.82	198.72	121.49
9	ENTERTAINMENT	125.48	49.74	63.74
10	TOTAL	=SUM(B4:B9)	=SUM(C4:C9)	=SUM(D4:D9)

A printout on paper showing the formulae can now be made in the usual way, using **File** and **Print** from the Excel menu or by clicking the printer icon on the Toolbar. Displaying the formulae in the cells causes the column widths to be greatly increased. In order to fit the spreadsheet onto as few pieces of paper as possible, it may be necessary to reduce the width of the columns, by dragging as described on page 93. It may also be convenient to print the spreadsheet in the **Landscape** orientation, as described below, rather than the normal **Portrait** orientation.

Landscape Orientation

Printing in **Landscape** mode effectively turns the paper sideways, allowing wider spreadsheets to be printed on a single page. To print in Landscape orientation select **File**, **Print** and **Properties** then switch on the **Landscape** button.

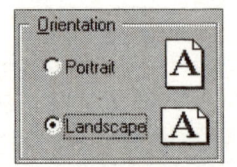

Exercise 9 - Creating a Spreadsheet and Entering Data and Formulae

The following exercise is based on the skills covered in the previous section and presented in the style of a CLAIT exercise. If necessary refer back to the notes if you have difficulty with any of the tasks.

You are to create a spreadsheet to monitor household spending.

1. Load the spreadsheet application.

2. Enter the title **HOUSEHOLD SPENDING**.

3. On a row below the title, enter the column headings below. **DESCRIPTION** should be left-aligned and the other headings right-aligned: **DESCRIPTION JAN FEB MAR**

4. Enter in the first column the following row labels, which should be left-aligned:

    FOOD MORTGAGE HEATING ELECTRICITY PETROL ENTERTAINMENT TOTAL

5. Enter the following numeric data:

DESCRIPTION	JAN	FEB	MAR
FOOD	247.87	259.25	238.31
MORTGAGE	494.36	494.36	505.27
HEATING	86.32	79.48	69.99
ELECTRICITY	39.78	36.45	31.98
PETROL	159.82	198.72	121.49
ENTERTAINMENT	125.48	49.74	63.74

6. Enter a formula to calculate the **TOTAL** spending for January.

7. Replicate this formula for the February and March totals.

8. Save the spreadsheet with a name such as **household1**.

9. Print a copy of the spreadsheet.

10. Display the spreadsheet on the screen showing all of the formulae used and print a copy on paper.

Editing a Spreadsheet

A spreadsheet will evolve over a period of time, to take account of changes in the data. The next section describes the *editing* of a spreadsheet and involves the following skills:

- Changing entries in the cells of the spreadsheet
- Replication of formulae down a column
- Deleting a row and deleting a column
- Adding a new row and adding a new column

Editing the Cell Contents

The method of editing a cell is basically the same whether the cell contains text (labels and headings), numbers or a formula.

The contents of a cell can be edited either by typing the amendment in the cell itself or by typing in the Formula Bar above the spreadsheet.

Editing in the Cell

To edit the cell contents in the cell, double click in the cell then manually type in the amendment. Press **Enter** to complete the amendment.

Editing in the Formula Bar

Click once in the required cell then click again in the Formula Bar. Manually type the amendment in the Formula Bar then click the tick to complete the new entry. If you are not happy with the editing, click the cross to undo the changes. The **Undo** icon on the Excel Toolbar can also be used to cancel any unwanted operations.

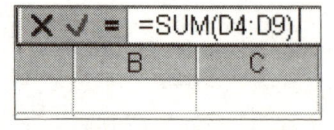

Totalling Along a Row

Returning to the Household Spending spreadsheet discussed earlier, we might wish to calculate the amount spent on each item - **FOOD**, **MORTGAGE**, etc., over the 3 month period. This involves totalling along each row of the spreadsheet in turn.

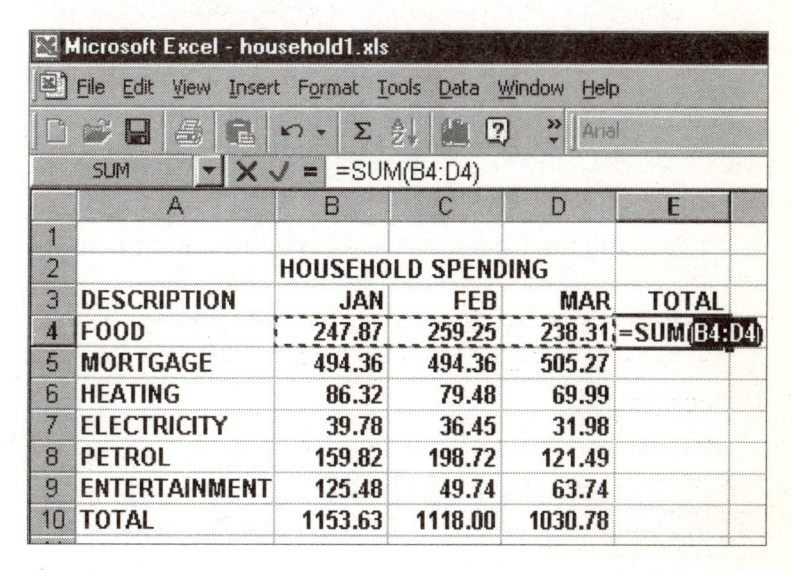

	A	B	C	D	E
1					
2		HOUSEHOLD SPENDING			
3	DESCRIPTION	JAN	FEB	MAR	TOTAL
4	FOOD	247.87	259.25	238.31	=SUM(B4:D4)
5	MORTGAGE	494.36	494.36	505.27	
6	HEATING	86.32	79.48	69.99	
7	ELECTRICITY	39.78	36.45	31.98	
8	PETROL	159.82	198.72	121.49	
9	ENTERTAINMENT	125.48	49.74	63.74	
10	TOTAL	1153.63	1118.00	1030.78	

First the label **TOTAL** is entered in cell **E3**. Then the formula to total along the **FOOD** row, **=SUM(B4:D4)** is entered in cell **E4**. This can be entered either by typing in the cell or by clicking the **AutoSum** icon on the Excel Toolbar.

AutoSum has a guess at the range of cells you want to total, as shown above by the dotted rectangle. In some situations this assumed range may not be what you intend, depending on the particular context, so check the range carefully. Then click the tick in the Formula Bar or press **Enter** if you are satisfied with the formula. Otherwise click the cross and redo the calculation.

Replicating a Formula Down a Column

We now need to repeat the row totalling for the other items of expenditure, **MORTGAGE**, **HEATING**, **ELECTRICITY**, etc. This means copying the formula in cell **E4**, but making the necessary adjustments to the cell references i.e. =SUM(B5:D5), =SUM(B6:D6), etc.

First click in cell **E4** and allow the cursor to hover over the bottom right of the cell (the **Fill handle**) until a small cross appears. Keeping the left mouse button held down, drag the cross down the column, over the cells where the formula is to be replicated.

> Drag the cross down the column to replicate the formula from cell E4 into cells E5-E10

After you release the mouse button the answers to the row totals appear in the cells, as shown below.

At the same time the **Auto Fill Options** smart tag appears on the bottom corner of the last cell in the range, **E10** in this example.

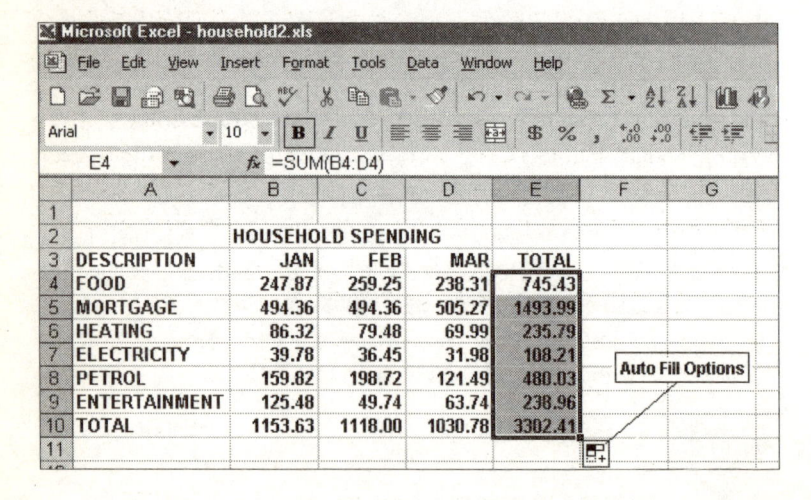

	A	B	C	D	E	F	G
1							
2			HOUSEHOLD SPENDING				
3	DESCRIPTION	JAN	FEB	MAR	TOTAL		
4	FOOD	247.87	259.25	238.31	745.43		
5	MORTGAGE	494.36	494.36	505.27	1493.99		
6	HEATING	86.32	79.48	69.99	235.79		
7	ELECTRICITY	39.78	36.45	31.98	108.21		
8	PETROL	159.82	198.72	121.49	480.03		
9	ENTERTAINMENT	125.48	49.74	63.74	238.96		
10	TOTAL	1153.63	1118.00	1030.78	3302.41		
11							

Auto Fill Options

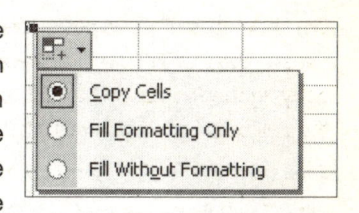

If you allow the cursor to hover over the **Auto Fill Options** smart tag shown on the previous page, then click the down arrow which appears, you are presented with the menu shown on the right. This gives several choices for the way the range of cells is to be filled. In this example **Copy Cells** is used to replicate the formula down the column, while adjusting the cell references. You can check this by displaying the formulae. Select **Tools**, **Options...**, **View** and switch on **Formulas** (as described on page 99). You should see the replicated formulae in column **E** of the spreadsheet, as shown on the right.

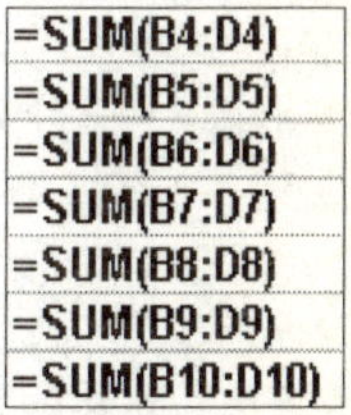

=SUM(B4:D4)
=SUM(B5:D5)
=SUM(B6:D6)
=SUM(B7:D7)
=SUM(B8:D8)
=SUM(B9:D9)
=SUM(B10:D10)

The other **Auto Fill Options** allow you to copy or replicate a cell or formula without copying the formatting, or to copy only the formatting. The above Auto Fill Options for copying down a column apply in a similar way to the task of replicating a formula along a row, as discussed earlier in this book.

Auto Fill and Series

If you use the **Fill handle** to copy a cell into a range of cells, Excel 2002 checks whether the cell being copied is part of a series. For example, entering **MON** into a cell and dragging it along a row will cause the Auto Fill smart tag to appear, as shown below. Among the options on the Auto Fill smart tag, the **Copy Cells** option would place **MON** in every cell, **Fill Series** completes the days of the week **MON** to **SAT** and **Fill Weekdays** completes the series using only the days **MON** to **FRI**.

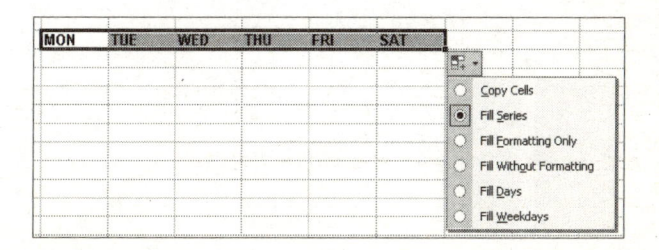

4 Using Microsoft Excel 2002

Deleting a Row

It may be necessary to delete a row from a spreadsheet; for example, to remove the **PETROL** row from the household spending spreadsheet.

Highlight the row by clicking in the box on the extreme left of the row, in this example the box containing **8** next to the label **PETROL,** as shown below:

Now select **Edit** and **Delete** from the Excel menu. The row and all of the cell contents are removed and the space previously taken by the row is closed up, i.e. no blank row is left. (If you select a row and press the **Delete** key, the cell contents are removed but a blank row remains).

Deleting a Column

Highlight the column by clicking in the column header, i.e. the box containing the column reference - **C** in the example on the right. Now select **Edit** and **Delete** from the Excel menu. This removes the entire column including the cell contents. The space previously taken by the column is closed up so that no blank column remains. (If you select a column then press the **Delete** key, the cell contents are removed but a blank column remains.)

Recovering from Mistakes

The speed with which you can delete rows and columns in Excel means it's also easy to delete the wrong row or column. If you make a mistake with any delete operation, the situation can often be recovered by *immediately* clicking the **Undo** icon on the Excel Toolbar. Alternatively select **Edit** and **Undo Delete** from the Menu Bar.

Inserting a New Row

When a new, blank row is inserted, it is placed *above* the row containing the cursor. Click anywhere in the row which is to be immediately *below* the new row. In the example shown below, the cursor was placed in the row for **ELECTRICITY**. Then you click **Insert** and **Rows** from the Excel Menu. A new, blank row is inserted ready for you to enter the new data.

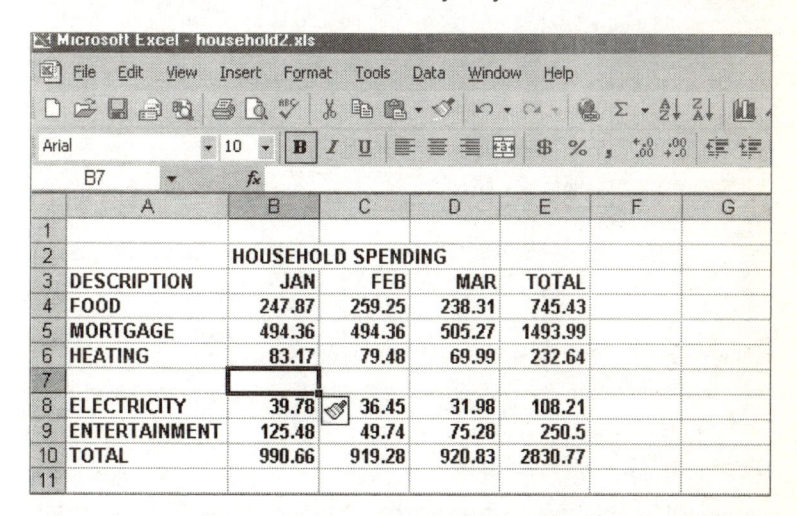

	A	B	C	D	E	F	G
1							
2		HOUSEHOLD SPENDING					
3	DESCRIPTION	JAN	FEB	MAR	TOTAL		
4	FOOD	247.87	259.25	238.31	745.43		
5	MORTGAGE	494.36	494.36	505.27	1493.99		
6	HEATING	83.17	79.48	69.99	232.64		
7							
8	ELECTRICITY	39.78	36.45	31.98	108.21		
9	ENTERTAINMENT	125.48	49.74	75.28	250.5		
10	TOTAL	990.66	919.28	920.83	2830.77		
11							

In this case Excel automatically adjusts the formulae in the **TOTAL** row to take account of the extra row **7** which has been inserted. So for example, the formula **=SUM(B4:B8)** originally in cell **B9** has become **=SUM(B4:B9)** in cell **B10**. Then when the new data is entered in the new row **7**, new values are calculated correctly in the **TOTAL** row **10**.

Formatting the New Row

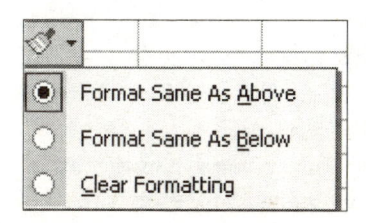

In cell **C8** of the above spreadsheet, the paintbrush icon represents a formatting smart tag. Hovering over this icon reveals a down arrow leading to the drop-down formatting menu shown on the left.

- Format Same As Above
- Format Same As Below
- Clear Formatting

Using Microsoft Excel 2002

Inserting a New Column

A new blank column is inserted to the *left* of the column in which the cursor is currently situated. Click anywhere in the column which is to be to the *right* of the new column. In the example below, the cursor was placed in the original column **E** headed **TOTAL**. Then you click **Insert** and **Columns** from the Excel menu. A new blank column **E** was inserted as shown below, ready for the new data to be entered.

	A	B	C	D	E	F	G	H
1								
2		HOUSEHOLD SPENDING						
3	DESCRIPTION	JAN	FEB	MAR		TOTAL		
4	FOOD	247.87	259.25	238.31		745.43		
5	MORTGAGE	494.36	494.36	505.27		1493.99		
6	HEATING	83.17	79.48	69.99		232.64		
7	ELECTRICITY	39.78	36.45	31.98		108.21		
8	ENTERTAINMENT	125.48	49.74	75.28		250.5		
9	TOTAL	990.66	919.28	920.83		2830.77		
10								

Formatting the New Column

In cell **F1** of the above spreadsheet, the paintbrush icon represents a formatting smart tag. Hovering over this icon reveals a down arrow leading to the drop-down menu shown on the right, presenting various formatting options.

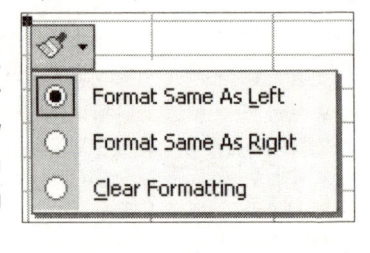

- ● Format Same As Left
- ○ Format Same As Right
- ○ Clear Formatting

After you enter the data in the new column **E**, the formula in column **F** is adjusted to allow for the changes to the spreadsheet. Mistakes can be undone using the **Undo** icon on the Excel Toolbar or by selecting **Edit** and **Undo ...** on the Menu Bar.

N.B. After adding or deleting rows and columns, check that all formulae are still correct. In particular, the cell ranges may need to be adjusted manually in the cell or in the Formula Bar.

Using Microsoft Excel 2002   4

Exercise 10 - Editing a Spreadsheet

This exercise covers the editing skills described in the previous section. Please refer back to the notes if you need help with any of the tasks.

1. Load up the spreadsheet saved in Exercise 9, with the suggested title **household1**.

2. Please make the following amendments: The cost of **HEATING** in January should be **£83.17**. The amount spent on **ENTERTAINMENT** in March should have been **£75.28**

3. Delete the row labelled **PETROL** to find the monthly spending without the cost of running a car.

4. Enter a label **TOTAL** on the right of **MAR**. Enter a formula to calculate the **TOTAL** spent on **FOOD** for the months of January, February and March.

5. Replicate the formula calculating the **TOTAL**, for each of the other items, **MORTGAGE**, **HEATING**, etc.

6. Save the spreadsheet with a name such as **household2**.

7. Insert a new column after **MAR** and before **TOTAL** with the heading **APR**. Enter the following data in the April column:

    FOOD £248.27, MORTGAGE £505.27, HEATING £59.32, ELECTRICITY £29.43, ENTERTAINMENT £84.36.

8. a Calculate the **TOTAL** for April.

    b Recalculate the figures in the **TOTAL** column.

9. Save the spreadsheet with a name such as **household3**.

10. Print a copy of the spreadsheet.

Formatting a Spreadsheet

Excel has many formatting features to change the way text and numbers are displayed in the cells. Some of the basic formatting effects are accessed from the Excel Toolbar shown below.

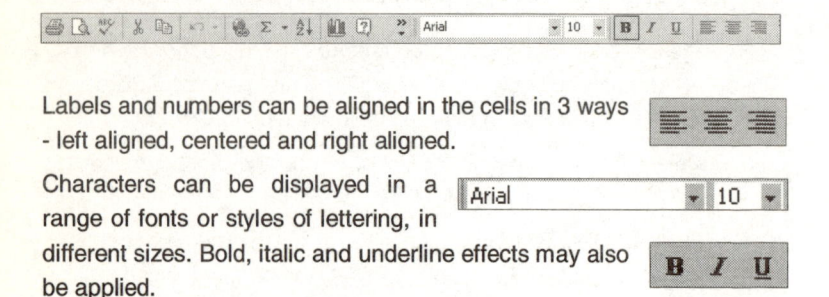

Labels and numbers can be aligned in the cells in 3 ways - left aligned, centered and right aligned.

Characters can be displayed in a range of fonts or styles of lettering, in different sizes. Bold, italic and underline effects may also be applied.

The general method is to select (i.e. highlight) the required cell or group of cells. Then select the required effect from the Excel Toolbar shown above. (Additional ways of formatting text and numbers are discussed shortly.)

Selecting or Highlighting Cells Prior to Formatting

Single Cell

Click anywhere in the cell.

Group of Cells

Drag the cursor over the required area of the spreadsheet.

Rows and Columns

Individual rows and columns can be selected by clicking in the boxes containing the numbers and letters for the cell references.

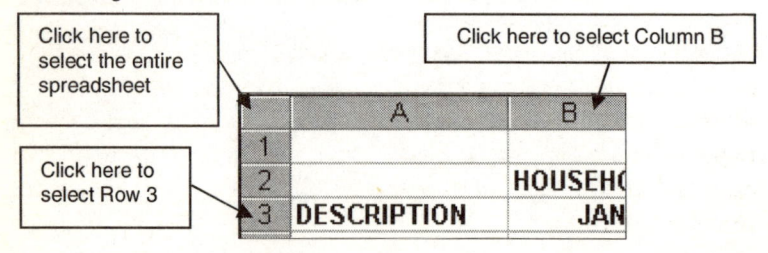

Click here to select the entire spreadsheet

Click here to select Column B

Click here to select Row 3

Applying Formatting Effects to Cells

Having selected a group of cells or the entire spreadsheet, various formatting effects can be applied using **Format** and **Cells...** off the Excel 2002 menu bar. Selecting the **Font** tag displays the following dialogue box, giving access to the entire range of styles of lettering.

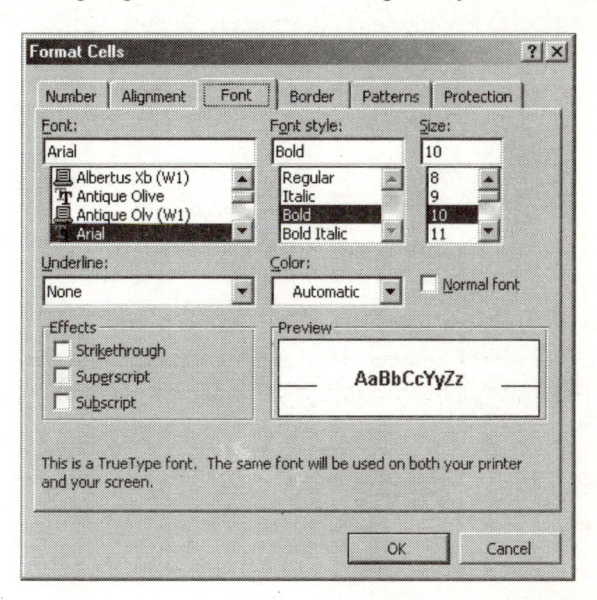

The **Patterns** tab shown on the right allows cells to be shaded in a variety of colours and patterns. You can also use the **Border** tab to select from a range of borders and internal gridlines in different styles. The **Alignment** tab allows text to be placed in various positions within a cell. In addition to **Left**, **Right** and **Centered**, text in a cell can be inclined at an angle specified by the user.

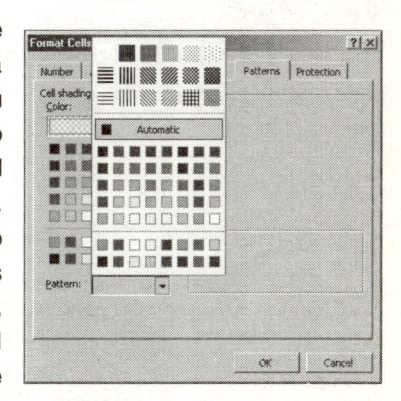

AutoFormat Options

Excel 2002 provides a set of ready-made spreadsheet designs or templates incorporating different fonts, shading and 3-D effects. These can be applied to all or part of an existing spreadsheet. After selecting the required cells, click **Format** and **AutoFormat...** from the Excel menu bar, to display samples of the formats provided.

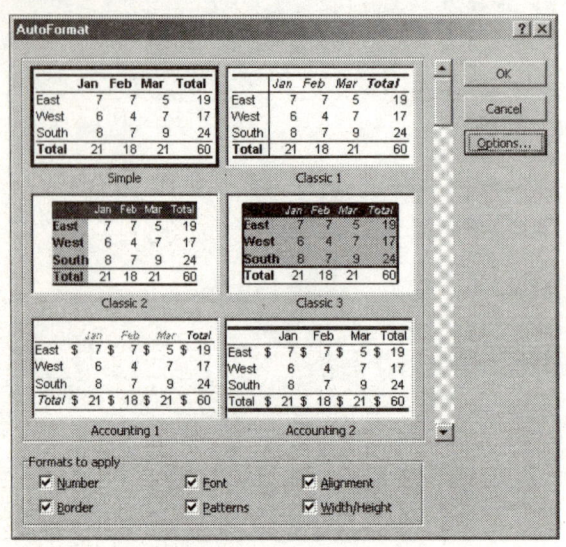

To apply a given format, click the sample to highlight it and then click **OK**. The **Options...** button presents the **Formats to apply** list at the bottom of the **AutoFormat** box shown above. This allows you to modify the given formats by removing some of the effects.

The Format Painter

The **Format Painter** allows you to copy the formatting in a cell (font, decimal places, etc.,) and apply it to another part of the spreadsheet. First select the cells whose format is to be copied. Then click the **Format Painter** icon, shown left, on the Excel 2002 toolbar. Finally drag the cursor (which changes to include a paintbrush) over the cells which are to be reformatted.

Formatting Numbers

Numbers can be displayed in several formats including *integer* and *decimal* as well as *currency* and *date*. To format numbers, highlight the required cells, then select **Format, Cells...** and the **Number** tab.

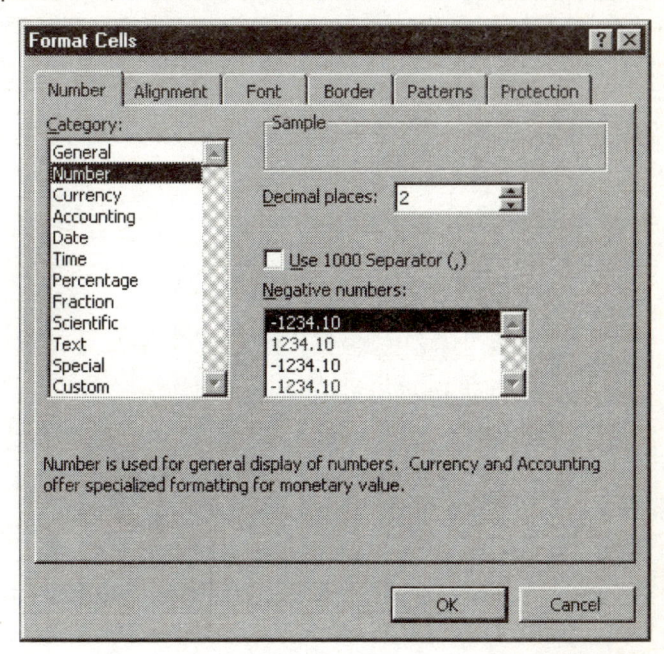

Numbers in Decimal Format

Numbers in decimal format are displayed with a decimal point and several figures after the point. For example, **29.87** has 2 decimal places. To format a set of selected numbers to 2 decimal places, select **Number** from the above **Category:** list and make sure the **Decimal places:** slot (shown right) is set to **2**, using the adjustment arrows. Then click **OK**.

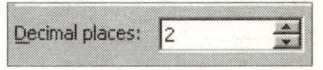

4 Using Microsoft Excel 2002

Numbers in Integer Format

Integers are *whole numbers* and therefore do not include any decimal places. The numbers **9** and **27** are examples of integers. To display a set of highlighted numbers in integer format, select **Number** from the **Category:** list shown previously. Then set the **Decimal places:** slot to **0** using the adjustment arrows. Finally click **OK**.

The last version of the Household Spending spreadsheet is shown below and includes some of the formatting just described.

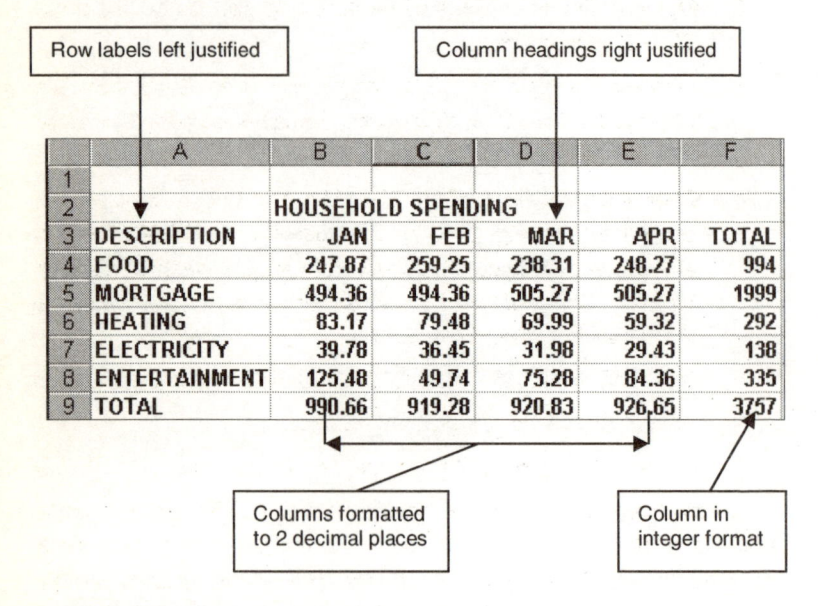

Row labels left justified

Column headings right justified

	A	B	C	D	E	F
1						
2		HOUSEHOLD SPENDING				
3	DESCRIPTION	JAN	FEB	MAR	APR	TOTAL
4	FOOD	247.87	259.25	238.31	248.27	994
5	MORTGAGE	494.36	494.36	505.27	505.27	1999
6	HEATING	83.17	79.48	69.99	59.32	292
7	ELECTRICITY	39.78	36.45	31.98	29.43	138
8	ENTERTAINMENT	125.48	49.74	75.28	84.36	335
9	TOTAL	990.66	919.28	920.83	926.65	3757

Columns formatted to 2 decimal places

Column in integer format

Numbers in General Format

By default, any numbers you enter into a new spreadsheet are displayed in the **General** format. This leaves the numbers roughly as you type them in, except that, for example, a number entered as **17.00** would be displayed as **17**, without a decimal point. The General format can lead to irregular columns of numbers with no alignment. Formatting to either 2 decimal places or integer format is often preferred.

Using Microsoft Excel 2002   4

Exercise 11 - Formatting a Spreadsheet

This exercise covers those features of Excel 2002 which allow you to change the appearance of a spreadsheet. All of the necessary skills are described in the previous pages. If you need help with a particular task, please refer back to the relevant section. The exercise is similar in style and content to a CLAIT practice exercise.

1. Reload the spreadsheet completed in Exercise 10, which you may have saved with the suggested name of **household3**.

2. Make a printout showing all the formulae used to calculate the **TOTAL** spending column.

3. Increase the width of the first column so that all descriptions are displayed in full. (Changing column widths is explained on page 93).

4. Display the data in the **JAN FEB MAR** and **APR** columns to two decimal places (e.g. 247.87). The figures in the **TOTAL** column should be displayed in integer format (i.e. without decimal places). (A copy of the spreadsheet with numeric cells formatted in this way is shown on page 114).

5. Save your spreadsheet with a name such as **household4**.

6. Print a copy of the spreadsheet on paper.

7. Exit from the spreadsheet application with data secure.

That completes all of the basic spreadsheet skills. On the next page there is a practice exercise covering all of the spreadsheet skills required for the CLAIT course. This is followed by a copy of the checklist of CLAIT spreadsheet skills, provided by Oxford Cambridge and RSA Examinations. You may wish to complete this list to assess your personal progress.

Using Microsoft Excel 2002

Exercise 12 - All Basic Spreadsheet Skills

This exercise is similar to a complete CLAIT assignment and covers all of the CLAIT spreadsheet objectives. You are to create a spreadsheet to calculate the weekly sales and income for bar meals sold in a pub.

1. Load the spreadsheet application.
2. Enter the title **BAR MEALS**.
3. On a row below the title enter the following column headings:

   DISH MON TUE WED THU FRI SAT TOTAL UNIT INCOME
                                                    PRICE

   The first column entitled **DISH** should be left aligned. The other headings should be right aligned.

4. Enter the following row labels, left aligned, in the first column:

   PIZZA SPECIAL
   COD AND CHIPS
   SEA BASS
   SCAMPI
   COQ AU VIN
   CHICKEN TIKKA
   TOTAL

5. Enter the data given below:

	MON	TUE	WED	THU	FRI	SAT	UNIT PRICE
PIZZA SPECIAL	4	3	8	9	12	17	4.95
COD AND CHIPS	4	7	6	14	23	21	5.50
SEA BASS	1	3	2	5	7	8	7.99
SCAMPI	3	2	6	8	13	10	6.50
COQ AU VIN	1	0	8	4	7	9	9.49
CHICKEN TIKKA	1	3	2	3	8	14	6.99

6. Save and print the spreadsheet.
7. Enter in the **TOTAL** column, a formula to calculate the total weekly sales for the **PIZZA SPECIAL**. Replicate this formula down the column to obtain the **TOTALS** for all of the other dishes sold.

8   **SEA BASS** is no longer available. To find out what effect this will have on sales, delete the row for **SEA BASS**.

9   Please correct the following errors. The number of **CHICKEN TIKKA** sold on Wednesday should have been 5.

   SCAMPI should have been entered as **WHOLETAIL SCAMPI**. Edit the row label. Increase the width of the **DISH** column to display **WHOLETAIL SCAMPI** in full.

10 Calculate the income from the **PIZZA SPECIAL** using the formula:

   TOTAL multiplied by **UNIT PRICE**.

   Replicate this formula to find the income for every dish.

11 Use a formula to calculate **TOTAL INCOME,** by adding together the income for every dish.

12 Save the spreadsheet and make a printout showing all of the formulae that have been used.

13 Insert a new row, **MUSHROOM RISOTTO**; between **WHOLETAIL SCAMPI** and **COQ AU VIN**.

	MON	TUE	WED	THU	FRI	SAT	UNIT PRICE
MUSHROOM RISOTTO	4	3	6	5	8	12	5.25

   Adjust the spreadsheet to show the **TOTAL** and **INCOME** from Mushroom Risotto. Recalculate the **TOTAL** income.

14 Display the figures in the **UNIT PRICE** and **INCOME** columns to two decimal places and all figures in integer format.

15 Save and print the spreadsheet.

16 Exit from the spreadsheet application with data secure.

Oxford Cambridge and RSA Examinations

Checklist of CLAIT Spreadsheet Skills

Objective	Achieved
3.1 Create a spreadsheet and enter data	
3.1.1 Initialise application	☐
3.1.2 Enter text	☐
3.1.3 Enter numeric data	☐
3.1.4 Enter formulae	☐
3.2 Edit and manipulate a spreadsheet	
3.2.1 Edit spreadsheet data	☐
3.2.2 Replicate entries	☐
3.2.3 Extend spreadsheet	☐
3.2.4 Generate new values	☐
3.3 Use spreadsheet display features	
3.3.1 Left and right justify text	☐
3.3.2 Change column width	☐
3.3.3 Use integer and decimal formats	☐
3.4 Save a spreadsheet, print contents and exit application	
3.4.1 Save spreadsheet	☐
3.4.2 Print spreadsheet display	☐
3.4.3 Exit from application with data secure	☐

5

Graphs and Charts

Introduction

When numbers are displayed in rows or columns in a table or spreadsheet, it can be difficult to see the underlying facts behind the figures. By presenting the numbers in the form of graphs and charts it's possible to interpret the figures at a glance. Graphs and charts enable previous results to be analysed and predictions made based on current trends.

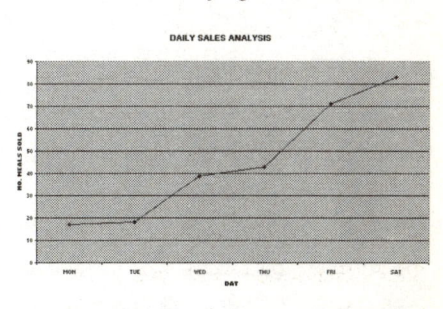

The Excel 2002 spreadsheet is a convenient environment for charting; first the numbers are entered into the spreadsheet in rows and columns. Then the **Chart Wizard** is launched by clicking its icon on the Excel Toolbar.

The wizard presents a vast choice of types of graphs and charts - pie chart, bar chart, line graph, etc. Then the wizard guides you through the drawing of the graph complete with labels, titles and scales, etc.

This chapter concentrates on the basic types of chart, i.e. pie chart, bar chart, line graph and comparative graphs. Skills with these charts are required for the CLAIT and IBT II courses offered by Oxford Cambridge and RSA Examinations.

5 Graphs and Charts

The Pie Chart

The pie chart shows how a total quantity is made up of a number of components, represented by sectors or "slices" of varying size.

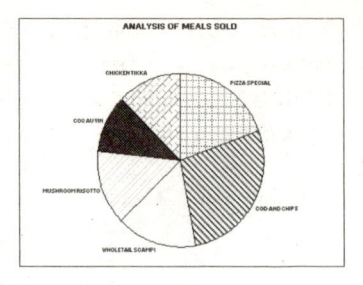

The pie chart facility in Excel 2002 allows the slices of the pie to be distinguished by different colours or different shading. You can also label each of the slices and add a title to the whole chart.

By default the slices of the pie are identified by a *legend* or key, shown on the left. The legend has been switched off in the above pie chart and instead the slices have been individually labelled.

The Bar Chart

The bar chart displays the columns side by side, enabling comparisons to be made. The bar chart below shows the total number of meals sold on different days of the week.

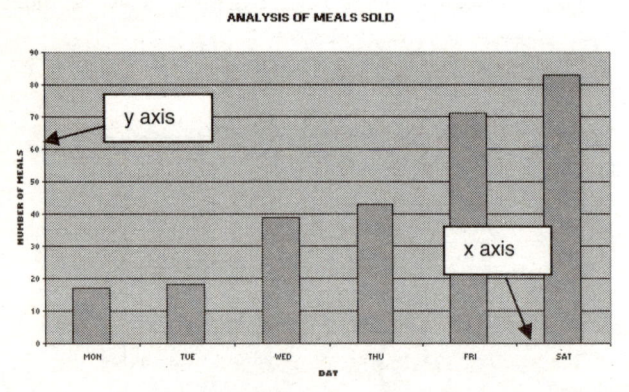

The bar chart should be labelled with a **chart title**, and a **title** and **scale** on both the **x axis** (horizontal) and the **y axis** (vertical). The bar chart normally displays *numbers* on the y axis and *categories* (days, years, meals or makes of car, for example) on the x axis.

Graphs and Charts

The Comparative Bar Chart

The comparative bar chart displays two or more columns for each category on the x axis. For example, to compare the number of **PIZZA SPECIAL** meals sold with the number of **CHICKEN TIKKA**, on different days of the week.

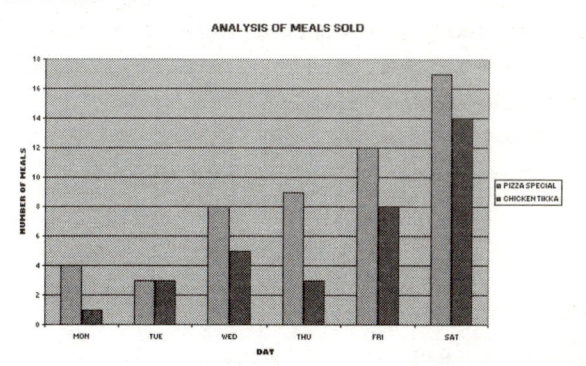

ANALYSIS OF MEALS SOLD

Note that a legend must be displayed on comparative graphs.

The Line Graph and Comparative Line Graph

The line graph is used to show how a quantity such as money or numbers of items sold (y axis), varies with time (x axis).

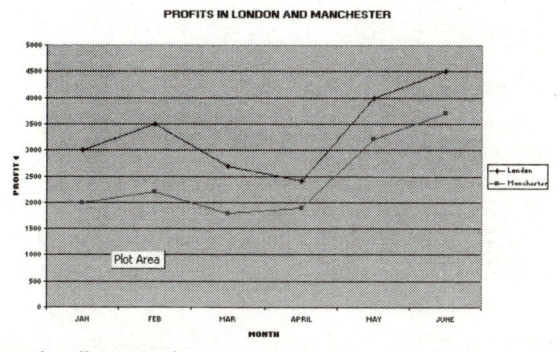

PROFITS IN LONDON AND MANCHESTER

The comparative line graph presents two or more lines on the same axes. The above graph compares profits in a London restaurant with those in Manchester. Again the legend is essential.

5 Graphs and Charts

Creating a Pie Chart

In this example, a pie chart is created to display the total number of bar meals served, based on the spreadsheet shown below. A pie chart will show at a glance which particular dishes contributed the most sales towards the total of **271** meals sold.

First we need to select or highlight two columns in the spreadsheet, as shown below. Column **A** will provide the labels for the slices of the pie chart while column **H** provides the raw numbers used to calculate the size of the slices.

	A	B	C	D	E	F	G	H
1								
2			BAR	MEALS				
3	DISH	MON	TUE	WED	THU	FRI	SAT	TOTAL
4								
5	PIZZA SPECIAL	4	3	8	9	12	17	53
6	COD AND CHIPS	4	7	6	14	23	21	75
7	WHOLETAIL SCAMPI	3	2	6	8	13	10	42
8	MUSHROOM RISOTTO	4	3	6	5	8	12	38
9	COQ AU VIN	1	0	8	4	7	9	29
10	CHICKEN TIKKA	1	3	5	3	8	14	34
11	TOTAL							271

To select a second column, hold down **Ctrl** and drag the cursor.

Selecting Two Columns Simultaneously

Select the first column (column **A**) by dragging the cursor over the required cells. In this case it is not necessary in column **A** to include the labels **DISH** or **TOTAL** in the selection.

Now select the required cells in column **H**. This is done by holding down the **Ctrl** key while dragging the cursor over the required cells. In this case the label **TOTAL** and the actual total **271** are not required in the block of highlighted cells.

Using the Chart Wizard

Start the **Chart Wizard** by clicking its icon on the Excel Toolbar. You are presented with a vast choice of different types of chart, from which we select the basic **Pie** chart.

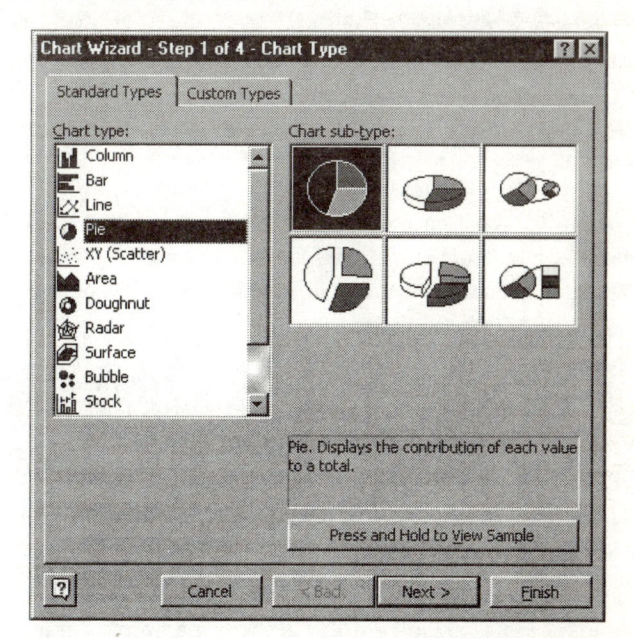

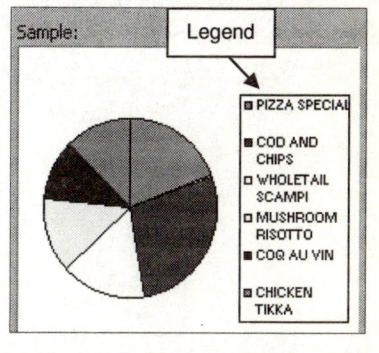

The button labelled **Press and Hold to View Sample** shown above gives an indication of the finished chart. However, as discussed shortly, there are various options, offered by the wizard, to tailor the way the chart is presented. For example, the *legend* shown on the right can be switched off. Instead the sectors of the pie chart can be individually labelled. It is also possible to apply patterns of shading to identify the sectors more clearly.

5   Graphs and Charts

After clicking **Next** you are given the chance to check the source data or "data series" for the chart. This means the ranges of cells selected in the original spreadsheet.

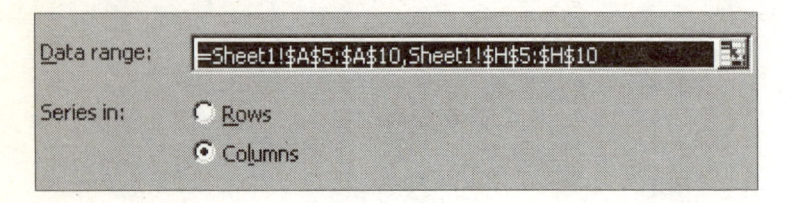

```
Data range:    =Sheet1!$A$5:$A$10,Sheet1!$H$5:$H$10

Series in:     ○ Rows
               ● Columns
```

In this example, ignoring the **$** signs, we have selected the data in columns **A** and **H**. The two data ranges are **A5** to **A10** and **H5** to **H10**. If these are not correct, they can be edited manually by typing the corrrection in the **Data range:** slot.

After clicking **Next** the wizard allows you to add a title for the whole pie chart. Make sure the **Titles** tab is selected and enter the title in the top slot, **Chart title:**.

Now select the **Legend** tab and switch off the tick next to **Show legend**.

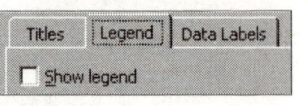

Then select the **Data Labels** tab and switch on the radio button next to **Category name** as shown below. This causes the slices of the pie chart to be labelled with the names such as **PIZZA SPECIAL**, etc.

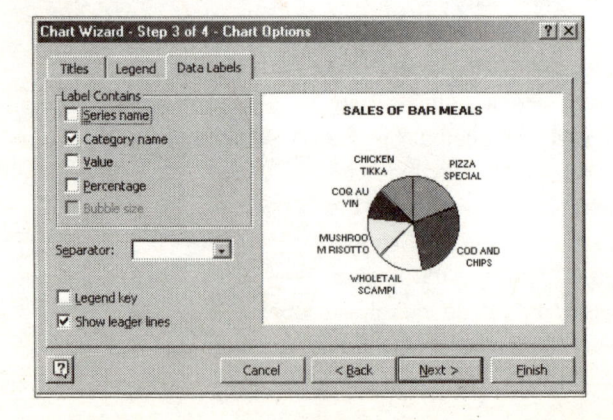

Graphs and Charts 5

The final stage of the **Chart Wizard** (after clicking **Next**) is the **Chart Location**. This determines the way the chart will be displayed.

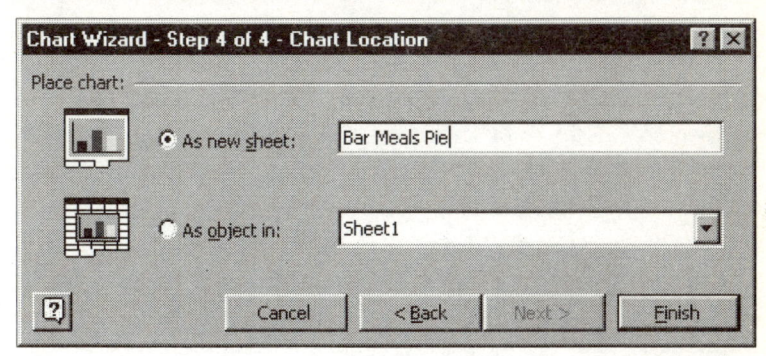

If you accept the default option **As object in:** the chart is embedded in the original spreadsheet which supplied the source data. This is shown on page 126. If you switch on the option **As new sheet:** the chart is displayed on a separate sheet as shown below. At this stage you can supply a name for the chart. This will appear on the tab for the chart at the bottom of the Excel screen. When you click **Finish**, the chart is displayed to the specification you selected during the various steps of the **Chart Wizard**.

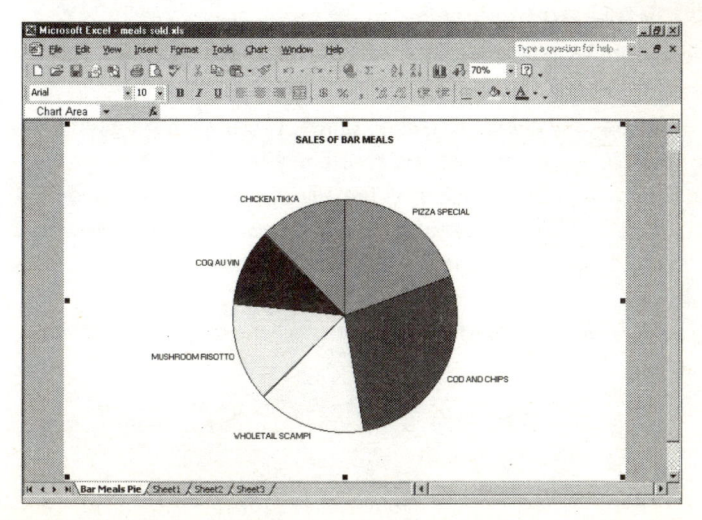

5 Graphs and Charts

Printing a Chart

A chart is printed using the normal **File** and **Print** options from the menus or by using the printer icon on the Excel Toolbar. By default the chart is printed in **Landscape** mode, i.e. so that the graph is viewed with the paper held sideways. Also, if the graph has been located so that it's embedded in the spreadsheet, then you must first select the **Chart Area** before printing. Otherwise the chart will be printed with the spreadsheet in the background, as indicated below.

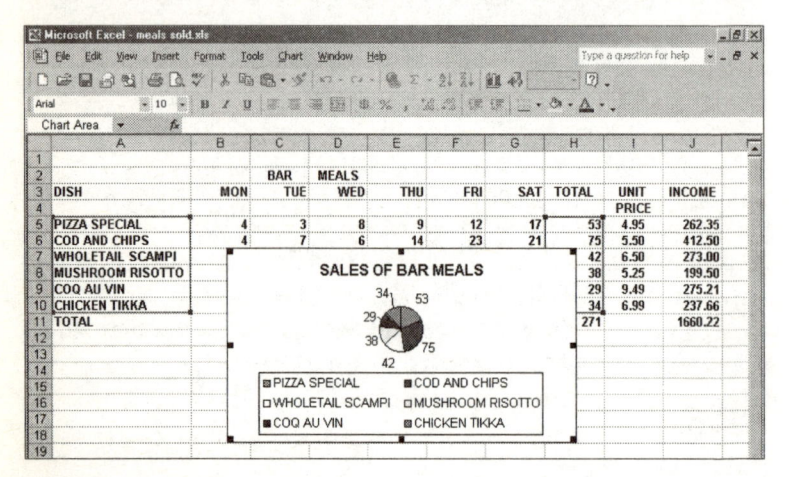

	A	B	C	D	E	F	G	H	I	J
1										
2			BAR	MEALS						
3	DISH	MON	TUE	WED	THU	FRI	SAT	TOTAL	UNIT	INCOME
4									PRICE	
5	PIZZA SPECIAL	4	3	8	9	12	17	53	4.95	262.35
6	COD AND CHIPS	4	7	6	14	23	21	75	5.50	412.50
7	WHOLETAIL SCAMPI							42	6.50	273.00
8	MUSHROOM RISOTTO							38	5.25	199.50
9	COQ AU VIN							29	9.49	275.21
10	CHICKEN TIKKA							34	6.99	237.66
11	TOTAL							271		1660.22

SALES OF BAR MEALS

(Pie chart with values: 34, 53, 29, 38, 75, 42)

- PIZZA SPECIAL
- COD AND CHIPS
- WHOLETAIL SCAMPI
- MUSHROOM RISOTTO
- COQ AU VIN
- CHICKEN TIKKA

Saving a Chart

No separate action is needed to save a chart. It is saved as part of the spreadsheet from which the data originated. When you save the spreadsheet, any charts are saved with it. However, it's a good idea to save the entire spreadsheet and charts regularly by clicking the disc icon on the Excel Toolbar. Alternatively use **File** and **Save As...** from the Excel menu bar if you want to save the spreadsheet with a different name. When the spreadsheet is subsequently retrieved, the charts are also retrieved. Moving between charts and spreadsheets is achieved using the **Chart** and **Sheet** tabs at the bottom of the Excel screen.

Chart5 \ **Bar Meals Pie** / Sheet1 / Sheet2 / Sheet3 /

Modifying an Existing Chart

As described on the previous pages, the **Chart Wizard** provides an easy method of creating a new chart. However, if you want to modify the chart later, select the **Chart** menu from the Excel Menu Bar.

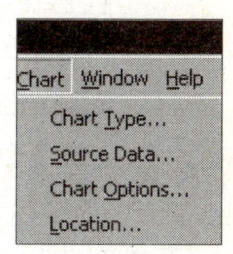

This menu allows you to revisit the options chosen during the various steps of the **Chart Wizard**. **Chart Type...** enables, say, an existing pie chart to be redrawn as a bar chart, for example. **Source Data...** allows you to change the range of cells used for the data. **Chart Options...** contains all of the options relating to the display of titles, labels and legends as described on page 124. **Location** presents a choice between displaying the chart embedded in the source spreadsheet or on a separate sheet, as described on page 125.

Changing the Patterns of Shading on a Chart

First double click over the required sector. The **Format Data Point** dialogue box opens, from which the **Patterns** tab should be selected.

Now click the **Fill Effects...** button and select the **Pattern** tab. A grid of patterns appears, as shown on the right. Select the required pattern and foreground and background colours, then click **OK** to apply this style the highlighted part of the chart.

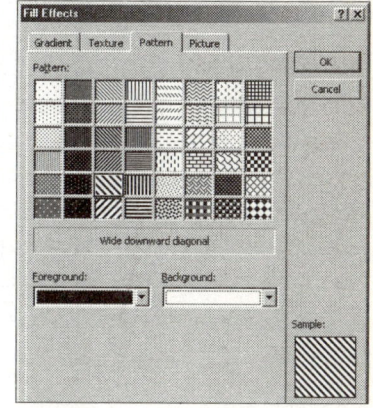

Repeat this process to shade all of the sectors of the chart. The same basic method can be used for filling in the columns on bar charts.

5 Graphs and Charts

Exercise 13 - Creating a Pie Chart

The following exercise is intended to give you practice in entering the data and creating a pie chart. Use the Excel 2002 spreadsheet to enter and save the data and use the Chart Wizard to create the graph.

Please refer back to the previous notes if you have difficulty with any of the tasks.

The exercise is similar to a Graphical Representation Of Data exercise in the CLAIT course from Oxford Cambridge and RSA Examinations. The data is entirely fictitious.

1. Load the application that will produce graphical representation from various sets of data.

2. You are going to produce a pie chart showing the number of cars of different makes owned by the residents of the village of Milbury.

    Enter the following data:

MAKE	NUMBER OF CARS
BMW	38
DATSUN	37
FORD	162
PEUGEOT	78
TOYOTA	41
ROVER	139

3. Save the data.

4. Create the pie chart including data labels for each of the sectors. Give the pie chart the heading **MAKES OF CAR IN MILBURY**.

5. Save the chart graphical display.

6. Print the pie chart including the required text.

Graphs and Charts 5

Creating a Bar Chart

The bar chart in this exercise is based on the spreadsheet below showing bar meals sold. The bar chart will show the total number of meals sold on the y axis. The x axis will show the days of the week.

	A	B	C	D	E	F	G	H
1								
2				BAR	MEALS			
3	DISH	MON	TUE	WED	THU	FRI	SAT	TOTAL
4								
5	PIZZA SPECIAL	4	3	8	9	12	17	53
6	COD AND CHIPS	4	7	6	14	23	21	75
7	WHOLETAIL SCAMPI	3	2	6	8	13	10	42
8	MUSHROOM RISOTTO	4	3	6	5	8	12	38
9	COQ AU VIN	1	0	8	4	7	9	29
10	CHICKEN TIKKA	1	3	5	3	8	14	34
11	TOTAL	17	18	39	43	71	83	271

This time the required data are in *rows*, **B3** to **G3** and **B11** to **G11**. Select row 3 by dragging the cursor over the required cells. Now hold down the **Ctrl** key and drag the cursor over cells **B11** to **G11**.

Now click the **Chart Wizard** icon and select **Column** (not **Bar!**) for the type of chart. Click **Next** and check that the **Data range:** is correct. Ignore the dollar signs.

Data range:	=Sheet1!$B$3:$G$3,Sheet1!$B$11:$G$11
Series in:	◉ Rows ○ Columns

Note above that the Data Series are in rows rather than columns. Click **Next** to move on to **Step 3** of the wizard. This enables you to add a title for the entire chart and to the x and y axes, as shown on the next page. Make sure the **Titles** tab is selected.

5   Graphs and Charts

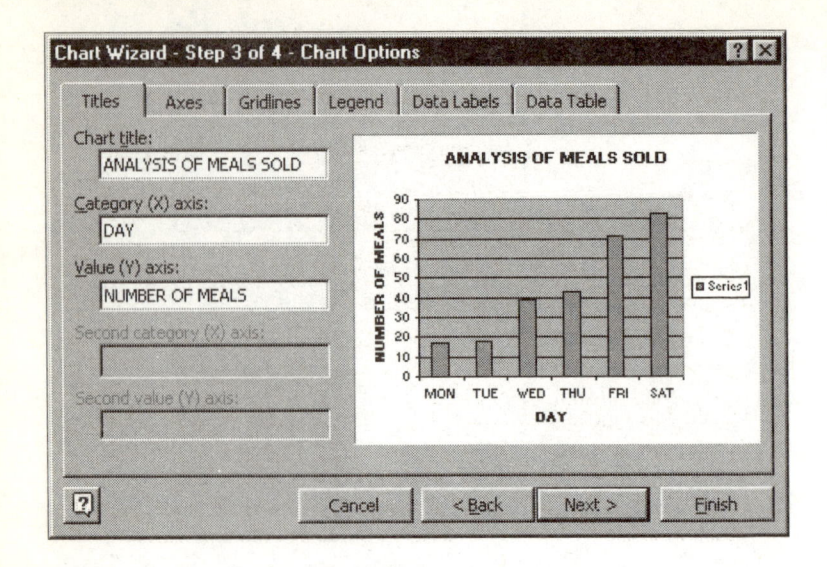

As this is a simple bar chart, with only one set of numbers (or Data Series) plotted, there is no need to show the legend. This can be switched off by selecting the **Legend** tab then clicking to remove the tick in the box next to **Show legend**.

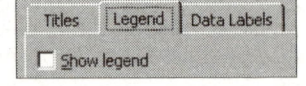

Click **Next** to move on to the **Chart Location**.

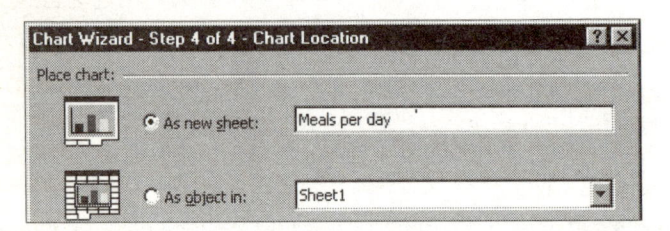

Select **As object in:** to embed the chart in the original spreadsheet. Select **As new sheet:** to display the bar chart on a separate sheet of its own. In this case type a meaningful name in the bar against **As new sheet:**. This name will appear on a tab at the bottom of the screen, allowing you to switch between the chart and the spreadsheet.

Graphs and Charts

When you click **Finish** the bar chart is drawn according to the options you selected during the various steps of the **Chart Wizard**.

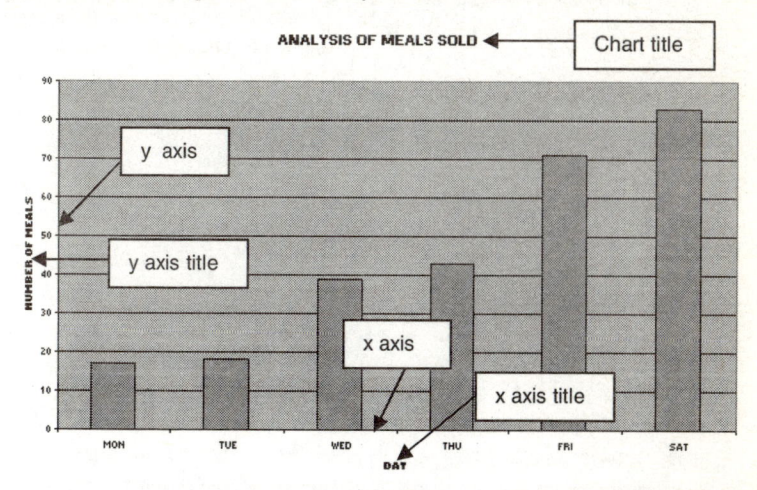

ANALYSIS OF MEALS SOLD — Chart title

y axis

y axis title

x axis

x axis title

Note the various titles. The legend has been switched off since it is not required on a bar chart containing only a single data series.

The settings for the bar chart can be altered using the **Chart** menu, more fully described on page 127.

Saving and Printing a Bar Chart

Please refer to the notes on page 126, covering the saving and printing of a pie chart. These notes apply equally to all types of chart.

Changing the Patterns of the Bars

Click once in one of the columns to select the entire data series. Select, from the Excel menu, **Format, Selected Data Series...**, then with the **Patterns** tab selected, click **Fill Effects...** and the **Pattern** tab. A grid of patterns appears. Select the required pattern and click **OK** to apply it to the highlighted data series.

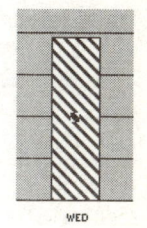

5 Graphs and Charts

The Comparative Bar Chart

In this example, we will compare the number of meals of each type served on Thursday, Friday and Saturday.

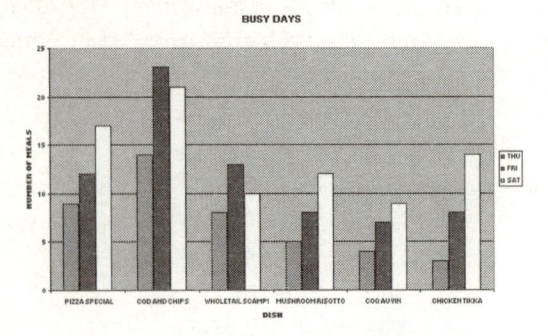

The names of the dishes will be displayed along the x axis. The number of meals served will be displayed on the y axis. For each dish there will be 3 columns, representing Thursday, Friday and Saturday.

	A	B	C	D	E	F	G	H
1								
2			BAR	MEALS				
3	DISH	MON	TUE	WED	THU	FRI	SAT	TOTAL
4	PIZZA SPECIAL	4	3	8	9	12	17	53
5	COD AND CHIPS	4	7	6	14	23	21	75
6	WHOLETAIL SCAMPI	3	2	6	8	13	10	42
7	MUSHROOM RISOTTO	4	3	6	5	8	12	38
8	COQ AU VIN	1	0	8	4	7	9	29
9	CHICKEN TIKKA	1	3	5	3	8	14	34
10	TOTAL	17	18	39	43	71	83	271

First select cells **A3** to **A9** as shown above, by dragging the cursor over the cells. Then hold down the **Ctrl** key and drag over cells **E3** to **G9**. When selecting the data, if you include the labels **THU**, **FRI** and **SAT** in the highlighted area, these will automatically be used as the labels for the legend on the bar chart. If you don't highlight the labels, the series names can be entered manually during the operation of the **Chart Wizard**. Now start the **Chart Wizard** and proceed as described in the previous section, in which a bar chart with a single data series was created.

Graphs and Charts 5

Since this is a comparative bar chart, it is essential that the three data series are identified with a legend. If you don't include the labels for the series when you highlight the cells on the spreadsheet, you can enter the names manually during **Step 2** of the wizard, in the **Chart Source Data** dialogue box. Select the **Series** tab then select **Series1** in the **Series** box. Enter the name of the first series **THU** in the **Name:** box. Repeat for **Series 2** and **Series 3**.

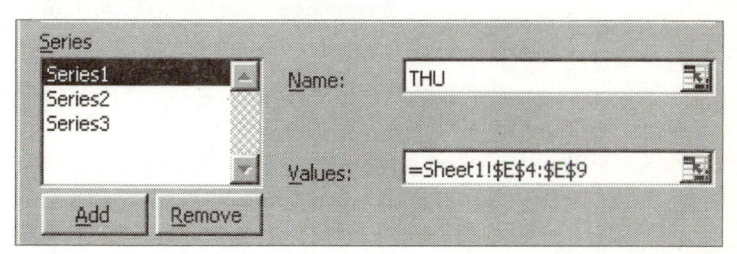

Follow the wizard through as described earlier for the simple bar chart. In the case of the comparative bar chart, however, do not switch off the tick for **Show legend**. The finished comparative bar chart is shown below. The three data series, i.e. the sales figures for Thursday, Friday and Saturday have been identified using different patterns as described on page 131.

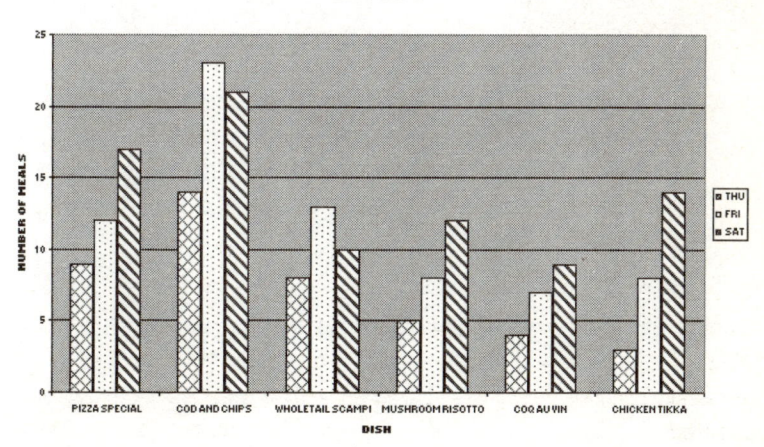

5 Graphs and Charts

Exercise 14 - Creating a Bar Chart

The following exercise is intended to give you practice in creating a bar chart. Use the Excel 2002 spreadsheet to enter and save the data and use the Chart Wizard to create the graph. Please refer to the previous notes if you have difficulty with any of the tasks.

The exercise is similar to a Graphical Representation Of Data exercise in the CLAIT course from Oxford Cambridge and RSA Examinations. The data is entirely fictitious.

1. Load the application that will produce graphical representation from various sets of data.

2. A comparative bar chart is required showing the monthly sales of motor cycles in a dealer's Bristol and Newcastle showrooms.

   Enter the following data:

MONTH	BRISTOL	NEWCASTLE
January	18	21
February	9	22
March	23	25
April	17	14
May	19	31
June	39	42

3. Save the data.

4. Create the comparative bar chart. Entitle the y axis **NUMBER OF MOTOR CYCLES** and entitle the x axis **MONTH**. Entitle the bar chart: **SALES IN BRISTOL AND NEWCASTLE**. Sales for the **BRISTOL** and **NEWCASTLE** showrooms should be identified by a legend.

5. Save the graphical display.

6. Print the comparative bar chart including the required text.

Creating a Line Graph

In this example, the sales of Pizza Special on the y axis are to be plotted against the days of the week on the x axis. A similar line graph for Mushroom Risotto is to be drawn on the same axes, making this a comparative graph.

	A	B	C	D	E	F	G	H
1								
2			BAR	MEALS				
3	DISH	MON	TUE	WED	THU	FRI	SAT	TOTAL
4								
5	PIZZA SPECIAL	4	3	8	9	12	17	53
6	COD AND CHIPS	4	7	6	14	23	21	75
7	WHOLETAIL SCAMPI	3	2	6	8	13	10	42
8	MUSHROOM RISOTTO	4	3	6	5	8	12	38
9	COQ AU VIN	1	0	8	4	7	9	29
10	CHICKEN TIKKA	1	3	5	3	8	14	34

The required data series are shown highlighted above. The labels **PIZZA SPECIAL** and **MUSHROOM RISOTTO** are included in the highlighting. These will be automatically displayed in the legend.

The method of creating a line graph is basically the same as that for creating a bar graph as previously described, once the type of graph has been selected at the start of the wizard. It is necessary to enter titles for the whole graph and the x and y axes. It is also essential to make sure the legend is displayed, as this a comparative line graph, i.e. 2 or more lines plotted are plotted on the same axes.

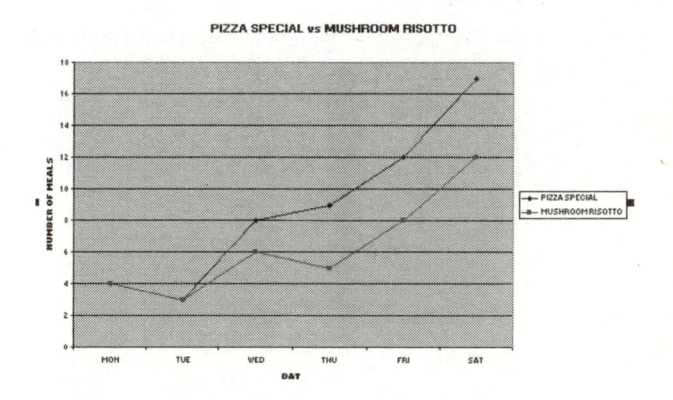

5   Graphs and Charts

Changing the Limits on the Vertical Scale

The range of values on the vertical or y axis can be changed, if appropriate. For example, the range on the graph below is initially **0** to **90**. It might be more convenient to alter the range to **10** to **100**.

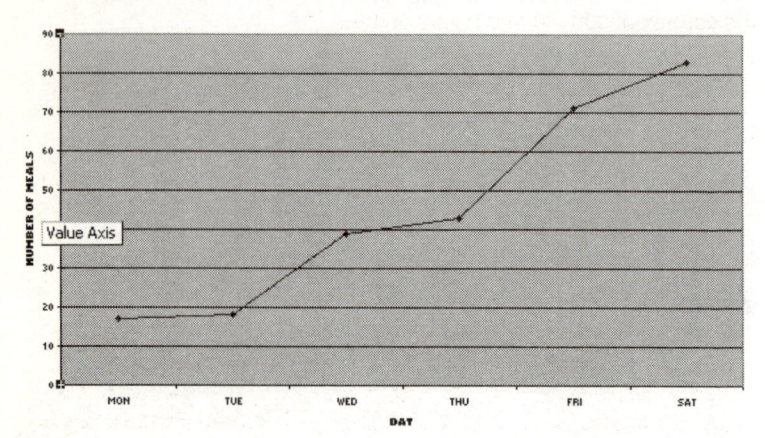

Allow the cursor to hover over the y axis until the label **Value Axis** appears as shown above. Then click the right button of the mouse. A small menu of 2 options appears from which **Format Axis...** should be selected. The **Format Axis** dialogue box appears. Now select the **Scale** tab, as shown below.

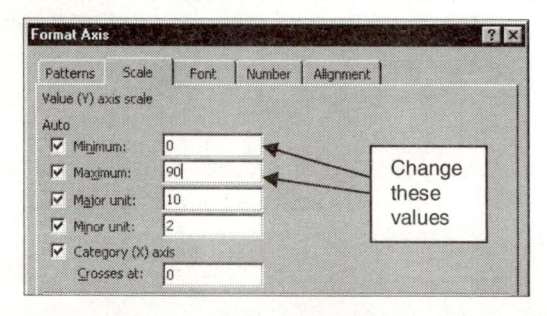

Replace the old values for **Minimum** and **Maximum** (0 and 90) with the new values (**10** and **100**). When you click **OK** the graph is redrawn with the new minimum and maximum values on the vertical axis, as shown on the next page.

Graphs and Charts

Changing the Size of a Chart or Graph

The overall dimensions of a chart can be increased or decreased by dragging with the mouse. Click in the **Plot Area as** shown below. The Plot Area should now be bordered by a dotted line with small squares at the corners and at the mid-points of the sides.

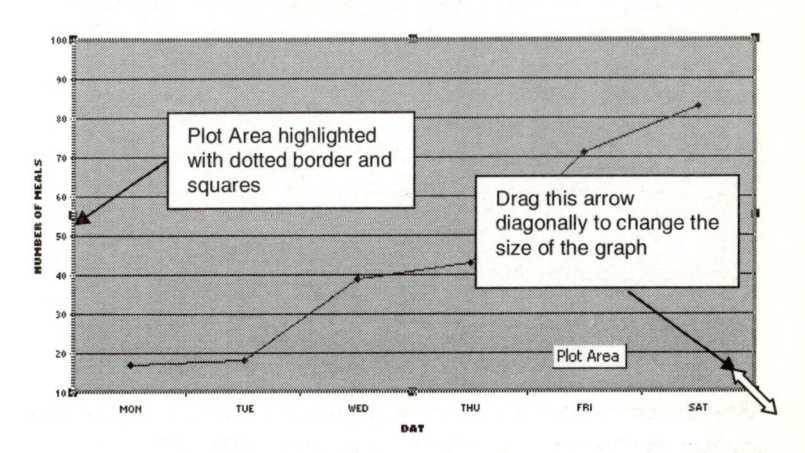

To reduce or increase the overall size of the graph, allow the cursor to hover over one of the small squares in the corner. An arrow appears as shown above. Drag the arrow diagonally inwards or outwards as necessary to change the size of the chart or graph on both the x and y axes.

Recap

This completes the basic skills needed to create the main types of graphs and charts. On the next page there is an exercise similar to a complete CLAIT assignment. It covers all of the CLAIT graphical representation of data assessment objectives.

The last page of this chapter presents a checklist of all the CLAIT graphical representation of data skills. You may wish to complete the checklist and perhaps revisit any skills which need more practice.

5 Graphs and Charts

Exercise 15 - Basic Graphical Representation of Data Skills

This exercise is similar to a complete CLAIT assignment and covers all of the CLAIT graphical representation of data objectives.

1. Load the application that will produce graphical display from various sets of data.

2. A bar chart is required to show the size of British Birds.

    a. Enter the following data:

BIRD	SIZE in centimetres
Starling	22
Chaffinch	15
Wren	10
Blue Tit	12
Jay	34
Woodpecker	32
Blackbird	25

    b. Save the data.

    c. Create the bar chart. Entitle the chart **BIRDS OF THE BRITISH ISLES**. Entitle the x axis **TYPE OF BIRD** and entitle the y axis **SIZE (centimetres)**.

    d. Save the graphical display.

    e. Print the bar chart including the required text.

3. A pie chart is required to show the percentage of total income spent by a family on different items.

    a. Enter the following data:

ITEM	% OF TOTAL EXPENDITURE
Food	21
Mortgage	36
Heating/lighting	11
Car	19
Entertainment	6
Clothes	7

    b. Save the data.

Graphs and Charts 5

    c   Create a pie chart including labels for each segment and the heading **SHARE OF TOTAL EXPENDITURE**.

    d   Save and print the pie chart.

4   A line graph is required showing the number of computers sold by a manufacturer.

    a   Enter the following data:

MONTH	Number of computers in thousands
July	4.5
Aug	3.8
September	5.5
October	4.9
November	9.1
December	15.4

    b   Save the data.

    c   Create a line graph. Entitle the x (horizontal) axis **MONTH**, and entitle the y (vertical) axis **NUMBER OF COMPUTERS (thousands)**. Enter a title for the line graph **SALES OF PERSONAL COMPUTERS**.

    d   Save and print the graphical display.

    e   Change the y (vertical) axis to display the range from **3 to 20 thousand computers**.

    f   Save and print the graphical display.

5 Graphs and Charts

5 A comparative bar chart is required showing the average monthly temperature for Sydney and London.

a Enter the following data:

MONTH	SYDNEY	LONDON
	Average Temperature (°C)	
January	22	4
February	22	5
Mar	21	6
April	18	9
May	15	12
June	13	15

b Save the data.

c Create a comparative bar chart and entitle the chart **AVERAGE MONTHLY TEMPERATURE**. Then entitle the x (horizontal) axis **MONTHS** and entitle the y (vertical) axis **TEMPERATURE (°C)**. The bars for **SYDNEY** and **LONDON** should be identified on the chart by legends.

d Save the graphical display.

e Print the comparative bar chart including the required text.

f Increase the size of the comparative chart on both the x and y axes.

g Print the resized comparative bar chart.

6 Exit from the application with all data secure.

Oxford Cambridge and RSA Examinations

Checklist of CLAIT Graphical Representation of Data Skills

Objective	Achieved
13.1 Enter data	
13.1.1 Initialise application	☐
13.1.2 Enter data	☐
13.2 Display graphs	
13.2.1 Display a pie chart	☐
13.2.2 Display a line graph	☐
13.2.3 Display a bar chart	☐
13.2.4 Display a comparative graph	☐
13.3 Control graphical display	
13.3.1 Control y axis scale	☐
13.3.2 Display the selected x axis range	☐
13.4 Save and print graphs	
13.4.1 Save data	☐
13.4.2 Save graphical display	☐
13.4.3 Print graphical display	☐
13.4.4 Exit from application with data and graphics secure	☐

5 Graphs and Charts

6

Further Work with Word 2002

Introduction

The previous chapters covered all of the basic skills needed for the various applications (word processor, spreadsheet, database, etc.) These skills are also relevant for the CLAIT qualification from Oxford Cambridge and RSA Examinations. However, the creation of longer documents requires additional word processing skills. These extra skills are also required for the Integrated Business Technology Stage II course from Oxford Cambridge and RSA Examinations.

This chapter describes the following skills using Word 2002:

- Changing the settings for:

    Margins

    Line length

    Indentation

    Paper size

    Character size

- Numbering pages
- Inserting page breaks
- The use of **Tab** stops
- The insertion of **Tables**
- Highlighting lists with *bullets* and *numbers*

The above skills will also be needed in Chapter 7 "Creating an Integrated Document". This chapter describes how extracts from the spreadsheet, database and charting applications can be integrated into the text in the word processor to create a large single document.

Setting the Margins

The margins are set from the **Page Setup** dialogue box, invoked from **File** and **Page Setup....**

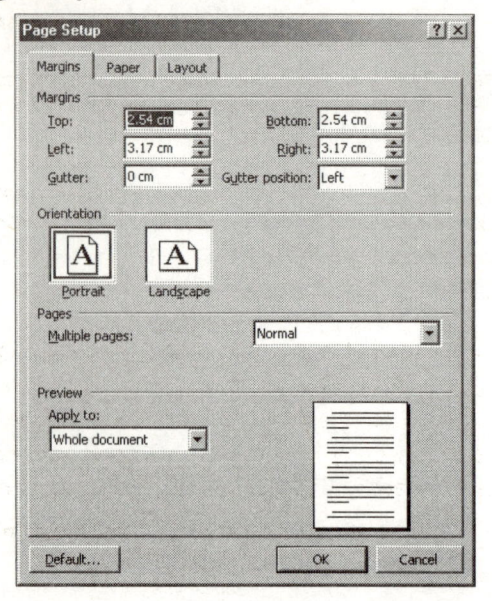

To change any of the margins simply delete the default value, e.g. **2.54 cm** for the **Top:** margin shown above, then type in the required value.

The left margin can also be changed using the Ruler on the Word 2002 screen. Drag the small arrows which appear when you let the cursor hover over the indent markers on the left-hand side of the Ruler.

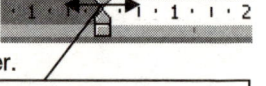

Drag here to change the left margin

Line Length

Word 2002 doesn't have a specific setting for line length. However, since the commonly used A4 paper size has a width of **21 cm**, the line length can be calculated using a simple equation:

left margin + line length + right margin = 21

Further Work with Word 2002 6

Indentation

Indentation involves emphasising a piece of text by locally increasing the left or right margin, as shown below.

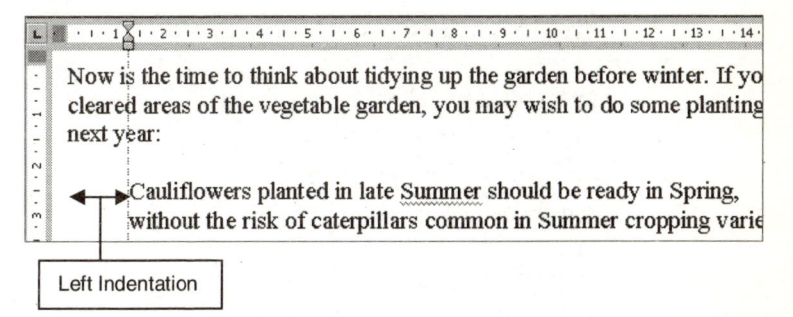

> Now is the time to think about tidying up the garden before winter. If yo
> cleared areas of the vegetable garden, you may wish to do some planting
> next year:
>
> Cauliflowers planted in late Summer should be ready in Spring,
> without the risk of caterpillars common in Summer cropping varie

Left Indentation

A quick method is to use the **Increase Indent** and **Decrease Indent** icons on the Word Toolbar, shown on the right. Place the cursor in the paragraph to be indented or highlight several paragraphs simultaneously, if necessary. Clicking the right-hand icon increases the indentation by 1.27 cm (½ an inch) for every click.

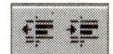

Alternatively drag the **Left Indent** (rectangular) or **Right Indent** marker on the bottom of the Ruler as shown below.

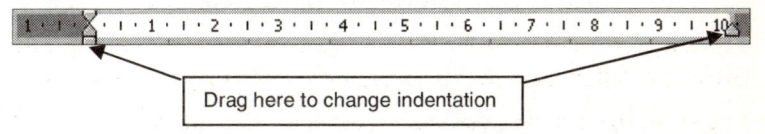

Drag here to change indentation

A precise way to change indentation is to highlight the text then select **Format** and **Paragraph** from the Word Menu Bar. The **Paragraph** dialogue box appears, into which the required indent value can be typed, as shown in the **Left:** and **Right:** bars below, under **Indentation**.

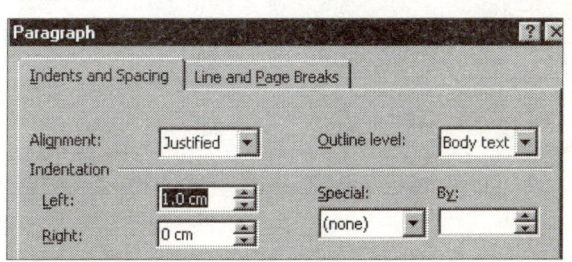

6 Further Work with Word 2002

Paper Size

When you start a new document in Word, the paper size is set at the **Letter** size by default. To change to the ubiquitous **A4** size, select **File** and **Page Setup** and click the **Paper** tab. If necessary, select a new **Paper size:** to match the actual paper used in your printer.

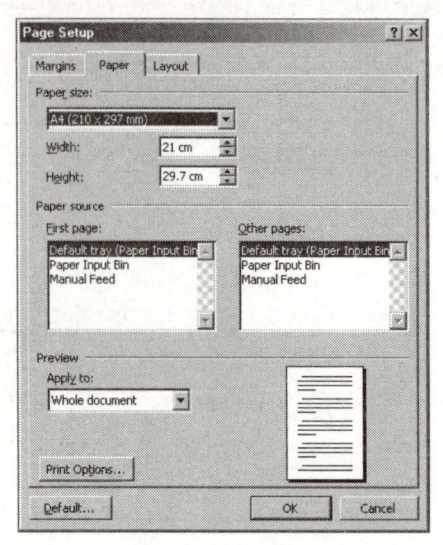

When you click **OK**, the paper size is changed to the newly specified size. The layout of the document on the screen will be adjusted accordingly

Changing Character Size

Many documents are formatted in the standard sizes of **10 point** or **12 point**. To change to a different character size, first select the piece of text to be modified. Then click on the down arrow to the right of the font size, (**10** in the above example). Then click the required character size. The selected text should immediately change to the new size.

Numbering the Pages

Page numbers are required on longer documents, such as this book for example. From **Insert** on the menu bar, select **Page Numbers...**.

You are given the chance to select the **Position:** (bottom or top of the page) and **Alignment:** (right, left, center, etc.) of the page numbers.

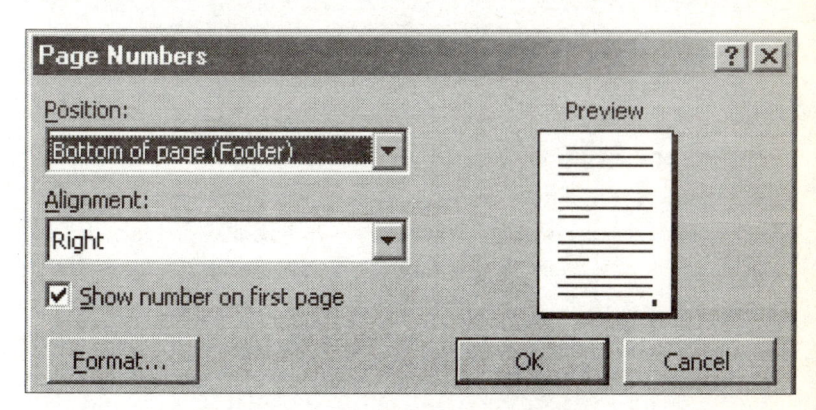

If you now click **Format...** you can type in a number for the first page (if you don't want the numbering to start at page 1). After clicking **OK** (twice) you are returned to the Word page, which should now display the page numbers as specified.

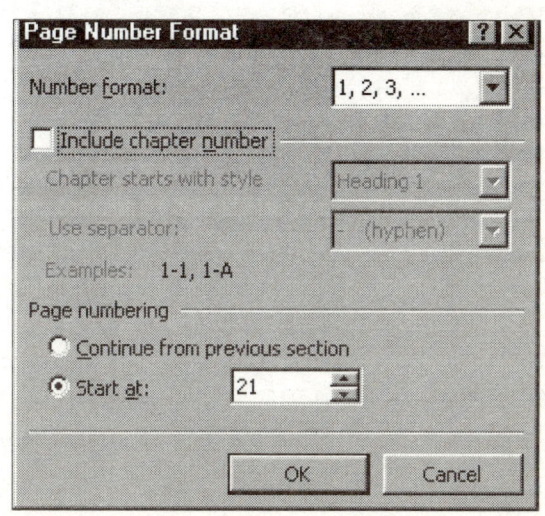

6 Further Work with Word 2002

Soft Page Breaks

When you reach the bottom of a page while typing, Word automatically jumps to a new page and inserts what is called a "soft page break". In **Normal** view this is shown as a line of dots across the screen.

In **Print Layout** view, a physical gap between two pages is shown.

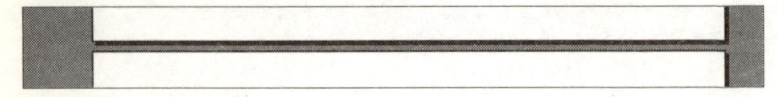

Hard Page Breaks

A hard page break can be inserted manually, anywhere on a page, whenever you want to start a new page. To insert a hard page break, place the cursor where the break is to occur and press **Ctrl** and **Enter**. Alternatively click **Insert** and **Break...**.

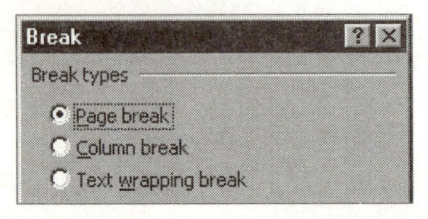

Then select **Page break** and click **OK**. The cursor jumps to the top of a new page.

In **Normal** view the hard page break is shown as a line of dots with the words **Page Break** in the middle.

....Page Break......................................

In **Print Layout** view the hard page break is not normally visible. However, if you switch on **Formatting marks** using the Toolbar icon shown on the right, the hard page break appears as a line across the screen, including the words **Page Break**, as shown above.

Deleting a Hard Page Break

Place the cursor on the left of the line of dots and press the **Delete** key.

Tabulation

The **Tab** is used for setting text and numbers in tabular form. These work in a similar way to the physical Tab Stops which are set manually on old fashioned typewriters. When you press the **Tab** key, shown right, the cursor jumps across to the next tab, a fixed position on the ruler, ready for you to begin typing. By default there are default Tabs set every 1.27 cm (or ½ an inch). If these settings aren't suitable, you can set your own Tabs by clicking in the appropriate place on the ruler. The new Tabs override the default ones.

First you must decide on the type of Tab required. The type of Tab can be changed by clicking in the small square to the left of the ruler. Some of the most common Tabs are listed below.

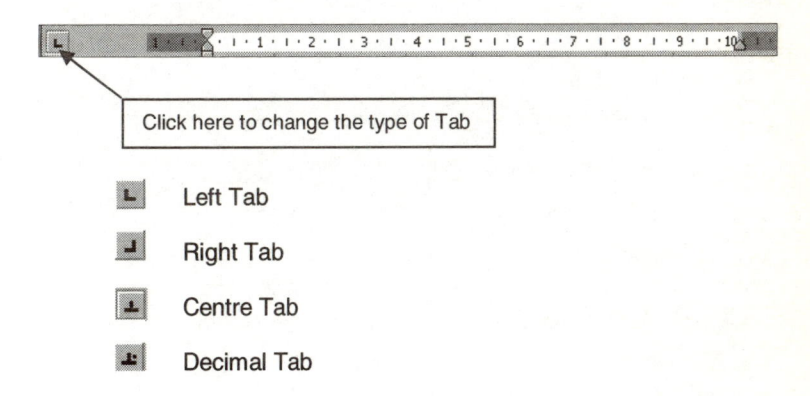

Click here to change the type of Tab

- Left Tab
- Right Tab
- Centre Tab
- Decimal Tab

When you've set the type of Tab, select the area of the document to which the Tab is to be applied, then click in the required spot in the ruler to insert the Tab.

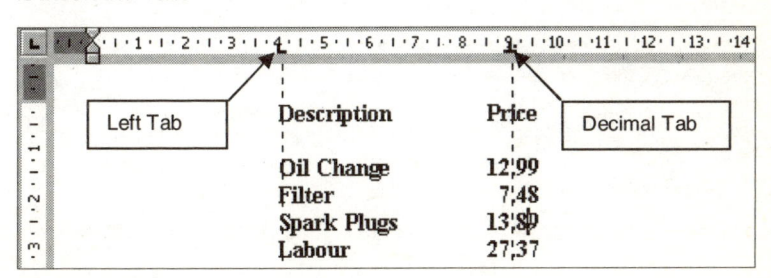

Left Tab	Description	Price	Decimal Tab
	Oil Change	12.99	
	Filter	7.48	
	Spark Plugs	13.80	
	Labour	27.37	

6 Further Work with Word 2002

The **Tabs** dialogue box accessed from **Format** and **Tabs...** allows Tabs to be set with greater precision than achieved when using the mouse.

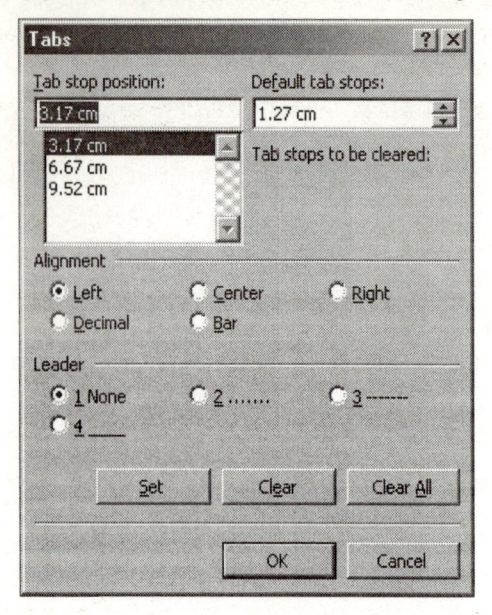

You can specify the exact position and type of the Tab, as well as clearing any redundant Tabs. The positioning of the default Tabs can be changed from the original setting of 1.27cm (or ½ an inch.)

The **Bar Tab** listed above inserts a small vertical line at the position of the Tab.

A **Leader** may be used to fill up the space before the Tab with a series of dots, as sometimes used in the contents pages of a book, for example.

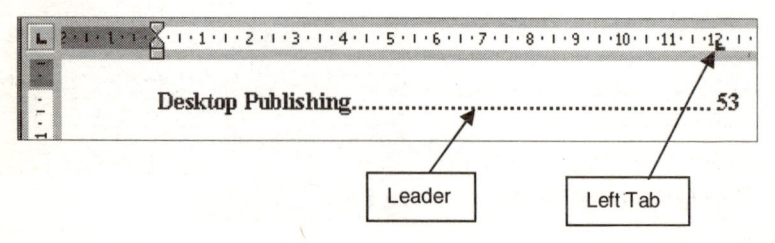

Further Work with Word 2002

Inserting Tables

The Tabs discussed in the previous section can be used for displaying data in simple tables. For more complex work, Word has a powerful **Table** feature accessed from the Menu Bar.

When you select **Table**, **Insert** and then **Table...**, a dialogue box appears allowing you to specify the number of rows and columns of the table.

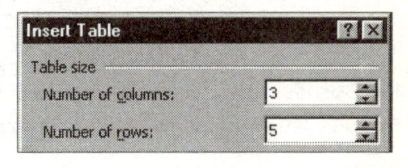

When you click **OK** the required table is inserted on the page at the current cursor position, as shown below. The table can be moved about the page by dragging the small square shown at the top left-hand corner of the table. Column widths and row heights can be adjusted by hovering over the lines and dragging the arrows which appear.

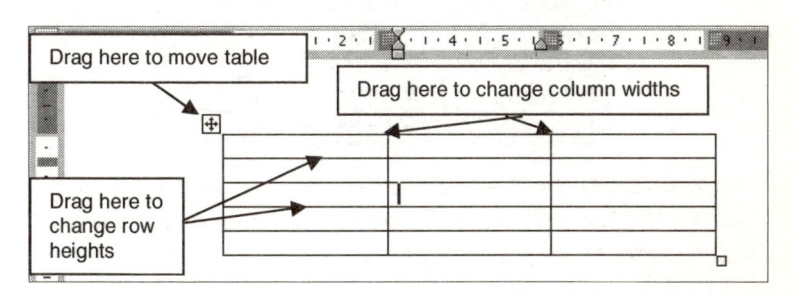

An existing table can be modified using the **Table** menu. First click inside the table then click **Select** off the **Table** menu. Rows and columns can be added or deleted. **Table Properties...** allows you to specify row heights and column widths by typing in precise values.

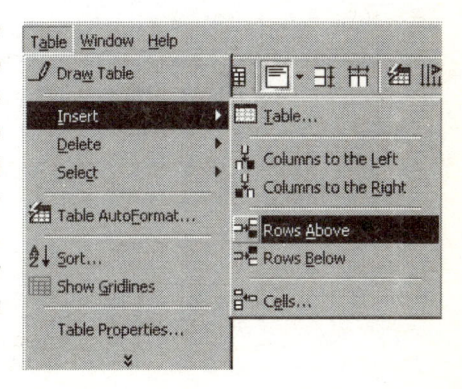

6 Further Work with Word 2002

Hiding Gridlines

There are options on the **Table** menu to **Show Gridlines** and **Hide Gridlines**. Selecting **Hide Gridlines** stops gridlines appearing in a table on the screen. It does not prevent the gridlines from printing on paper.

To print a table on paper without gridlines, click inside the table. Then from the Menu Bar select **Format**, **Borders and Shading...** and click the **Borders** tab. Under **Setting:** click in the square next to **None**. Click **OK** and the gridlines will no longer appear when the table is printed on paper.

Bullets and Numbering

These two features are both used to emphasise lists and are applied in a similar way. To apply either effect, highlight the required piece of text and then select **Format** and **Bullets and Numbering...** from the Menu Bar. Alternatively click one of the icons shown on the right, from the Word Toolbar.

- 4 Bedrooms
- 2 Bathrooms
- Large Garden
- Double Garage
- Rural Situation

1. Research
2. Draft
3. Editing
4. Proof Reading
5. Printing

If you select **Bullets and Numbering...** from the **Format** menu, you can choose from a large range of styles, as shown on the right. **Customize...** opens a window which allows you to change the size of the bullets and numbers and the size of the indents of the bullets and numbers and the text.

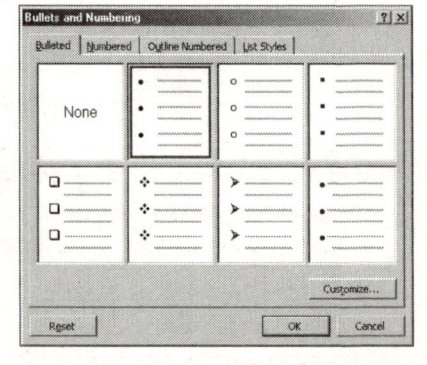

7
Creating an Integrated Document

Introduction

So far this book has considered, in isolation, the four main applications - word processor, database, spreadsheet and graphs and charts. However, when producing a substantial report, it's likely that information from several applications will need to be integrated into a single document. A student project or dissertation, for example, produced in a word processor, may well need to include extracts from a spreadsheet, a database and a charting program. This task is now relatively simple, with *integrated software* such as Microsoft Office XP, designed to ease the transfer of information between applications.

Multitasking

To transfer extracts from the spreadsheet, database and charts into a Word document, it's necessary for the relevant programs to be running in the computer at the same time - a process known as *multitasking*.

For example, to place an extract from the Excel spreadsheet into Word, start Word running with the required document open on the screen. Then Excel is started while Word continues running in the background. The programs currently running in the computer are indicated by icons on the Windows Taskbar at the bottom of the screen.

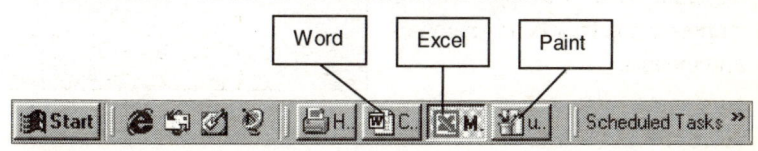

In the previous example, the icons represent, reading from left to right, Word, Excel and Paint. To display fully on the screen any of the programs currently running in the background, click the program's icon on the Taskbar. The program opens up to fill the entire screen. To *minimise* a program which currently fills the screen, again click its icon on the Taskbar.

Alternatively hold down the **Alt** key and repeatedly press the **Tab** key to "cycle" through the programs currently running. The names of the programs are displayed in a small window. Release the keys to display the program currently listed in the window.

Importing Extracts from Other Applications into Word

The general method is to type the basic framework of the report in Word 2002. Then, *while still running Word*, open up the relevant application, such as the Excel spreadsheet or Access database. The required extract from the spreadsheet, for example, is selected on the screen, then copied and pasted into Word. This can be repeated with extracts from the Access database or graphs produced in the Excel Chart Wizard, as required. Finally, the entire integrated document, including the various extracts, can be saved and printed as a single Word file.

The following pages cover the creation of an integrated document. The amount of data used is limited compared with a real situation. This should allow you to follow the work as an exercise at the computer and to concentrate on the new skills involved.

The Basic Word Document

It's a good idea to use the same font and character size throughout the work, in the word processor, database, spreadsheet, etc. Common fonts for reports are Times New Roman or Arial size 10 or 12. Page numbers and margins, etc., should be set at the start and these were discussed in the previous chapter. You may wish to enter the data for this fictitious business report as an exercise in creating an integrated document.

Creating an Integrated Document 7

Inserting a Spreadsheet Extract into a Word Document

Setting the Insertion Point in Word

With the word processing document open on the screen, the cursor is placed at the point where the top left-hand corner of the spreadsheet is to appear.

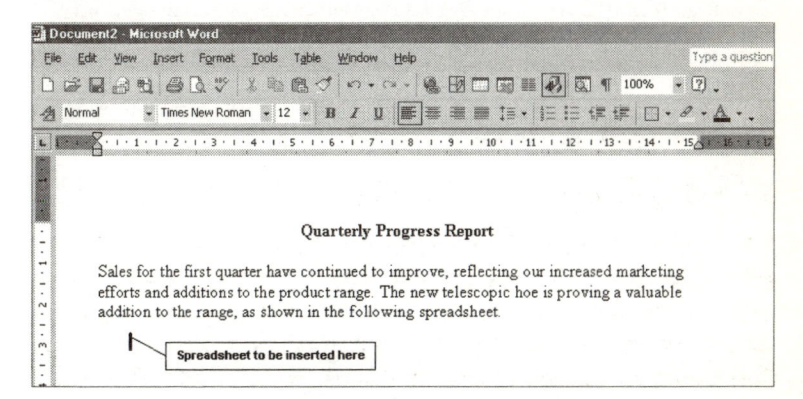

Quarterly Progress Report

Sales for the first quarter have continued to improve, reflecting our increased marketing efforts and additions to the product range. The new telescopic hoe is proving a valuable addition to the range, as shown in the following spreadsheet.

Spreadsheet to be inserted here

Copying a Spreadsheet Extract to the Clipboard

Now, with the word processor still running, the spreadsheet program Excel 2002 is launched from **Start, Programs** and **Microsoft Excel**. The spreadsheet program starts up and Word 2002 disappears into the background. With Excel running on the screen you now need to retrieve the required spreadsheet file from the hard disc. Alternatively, for the purposes of this exercise, you may wish to type in the simple spreadsheet shown below.

	A	B	C	D	E
1			SALES £		
2	PRODUCT	JAN	FEB	MAR	TOTAL
3	Forks	3569.97	4376.56	4182.58	12129.11
4	Spades	4689.21	6294.34	2398.76	13382.31
5	Wheelbarrow	3693.79	4287.39	5187.17	13168.35
6	Rakes	1845.31	2398.54	397.55	4641.40
7	Secateurs	948.32	1243.98	1000.76	3193.06
8	Hoes	2389.42	2876.34	3789.99	9055.75

7   Creating an Integrated Document

Now highlight, by dragging with the mouse, the area of the spreadsheet you wish to include in the document in the word processor. The extract can be the whole spreadsheet or just a small area consisting of a few cells.

Task Panes and the Clipboard

Select **Edit** and **Copy** from the Excel Menu Bar. Alternatively click the **Copy** icon on the Excel 2002 Toolbar. The **Copy** operation places the spreadsheet extract onto the *clipboard,* a temporary holding area in the computer's memory. With the introduction of Task Panes, Microsoft Office XP allows you to see a list of the items stored on the clipboard. The Task Pane appears on the right of the Excel screen, as shown below. The clipboard contents can be viewed in the Task Pane by selecting **Edit** and **Office Clipboard...**. Alternatively hold down **Ctrl** and press the **C** key twice. The clipboard contents are shown in the Task Pane on the right of the screenshot below.

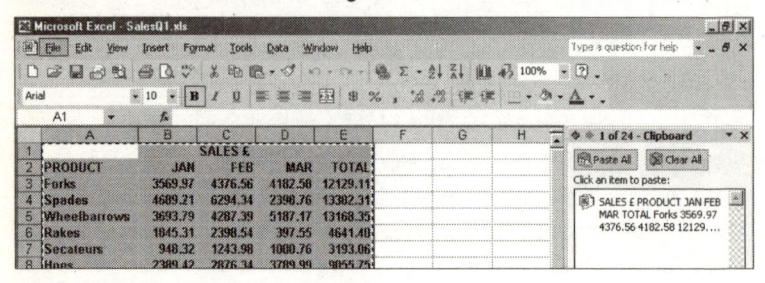

The Task Pane now shows the items you have copied to the clipboard. The screenshot above shows the spreadsheet extract highlighted, with a copy stored on the clipboard. The clipboard shows a summary of the spreadsheet extract. Clicking the down arrow to the right of the summary reveals a small menu with options to **Paste** or **Delete** the extract, as shown on the right.

The contents displayed in the clipboard window of the Task Pane stay the same whether viewed from Microsoft Word, Excel or Access.

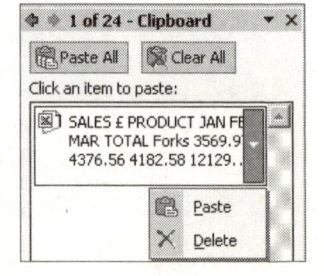

156

Creating an Integrated Document 7

Pasting the Spreadsheet Extract into Word

Switch back to Word by clicking its icon on the Windows Toolbar or by holding down **Alt** and pressing **Tab**, then releasing when Word is highlighted. The clipboard contents can be viewed in Word in the Task Pane by selecting **Edit** and **Office Clipboard...**. Alternatively hold down **Ctrl** and press the **C** key twice. Make sure the cursor in the Word document is at the required insertion point for the top left-hand corner of the spreadsheet extract. Now, working within the clipboard window of the Task pane, click the entry for the spreadsheet extract. The spreadsheet extract is pasted into the Word document at the insertion point, as shown below.

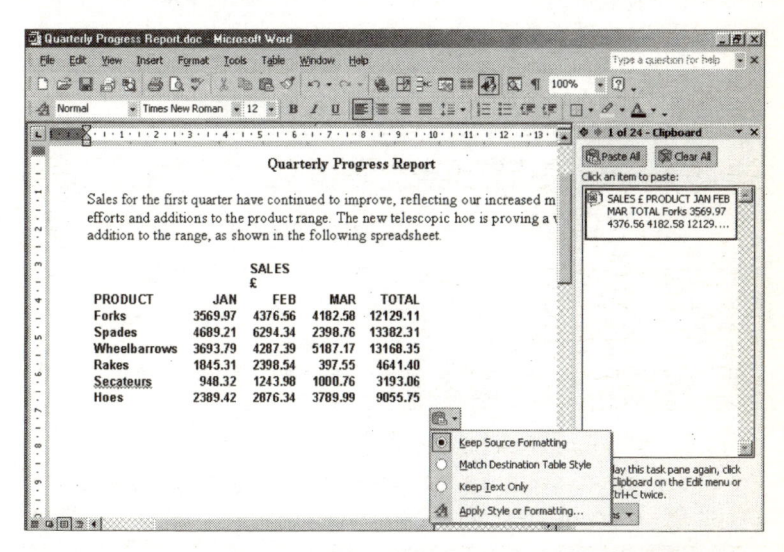

The pasting smart tag appears at the bottom right of the spreadsheet extract, as shown above. Clicking the down arrow on the right of the smart tag opens a drop-down menu giving various formatting options for the spreadsheet extract in its new situation on the Word 2002 page. These allow you to keep the original Excel (source) format of the spreadsheet extract or change to a new style.

7　Creating an Integrated Document

Advantages of the Task Pane

The above paste operation could be achieved by selecting **Edit** and **Paste** from the Menu Bar or by clicking the **Paste** icon on the Word Toolbar, without using the Task Pane. However, the clipboard window in the Task Pane makes it easy to manage a large number of items which have been copied to the clipboard. Each item is represented by a clear listing or a thumbnail picture so that it's easy to select the correct one for pasting into a given location. Tasks such as deleting individual items or clearing the clipboard are also made easier by the use of the Task Pane.

Moving a Spreadsheet Extract within a Word Document

Allow the cursor to hover over the spreadsheet area until squares appear at the top left and bottom right of the sheet, as shown below. Drag the square at the top left to move the spreadsheet extract to a new position.

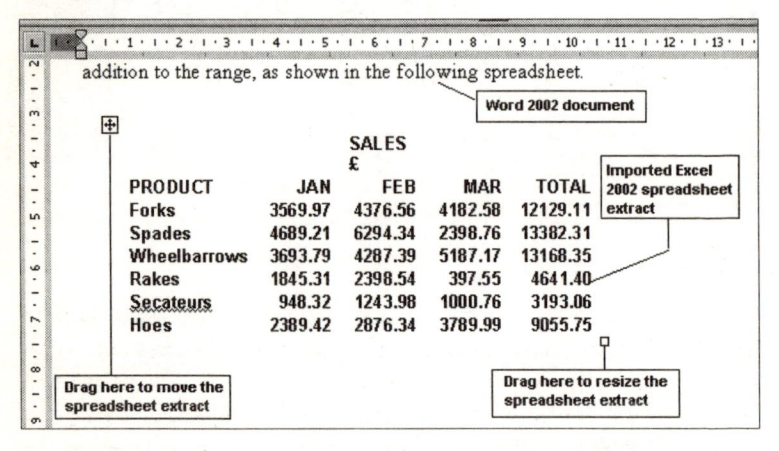

addition to the range, as shown in the following spreadsheet.

Word 2002 document

PRODUCT	JAN	FEB	MAR	TOTAL
Forks	3569.97	4376.56	4182.58	12129.11
Spades	4689.21	6294.34	2398.76	13382.31
Wheelbarrows	3693.79	4287.39	5187.17	13168.35
Rakes	1845.31	2398.54	397.55	4641.40
Secateurs	948.32	1243.98	1000.76	3193.06
Hoes	2389.42	2876.34	3789.99	9055.75

SALES £

Imported Excel 2002 spreadsheet extract

Drag here to move the spreadsheet extract

Drag here to resize the spreadsheet extract

Resizing a Spreadsheet Extract within a Word Document

To adjust the size of the spreadsheet extract, drag the small square at the bottom right of the spreadsheet extract, as shown above.

Saving an Integrated Document

Save the Word document in the normal way. The spreadsheet extract will be saved as an integral part of the Word document.

Creating an Integrated Document 7

Inserting a Graph or Chart into a Word Document

In the following example a pie chart is used, but the basic method of inserting a chart is the same for all types of charts and graphs.

Setting the Insertion Point in Word

With Word running and the required document open on the screen, the cursor is placed at the insertion point for the top left-hand corner of the chart frame.

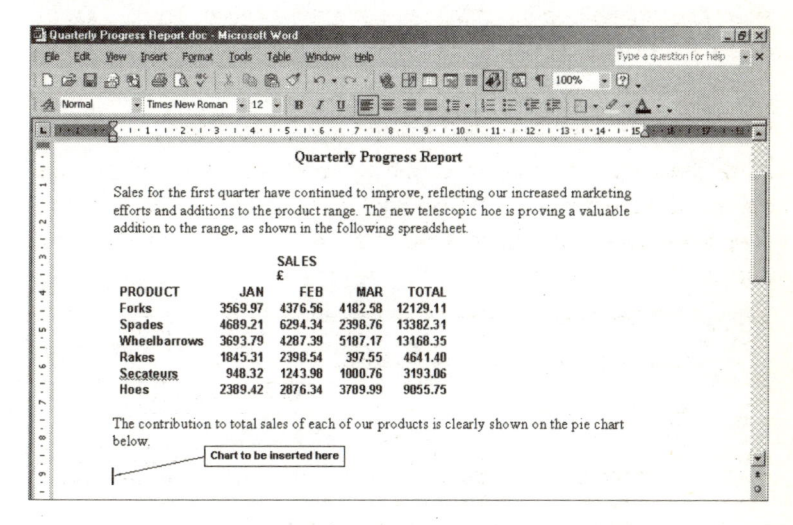

Preparing the Pie Chart

While still running Word, start up Excel and load up the required chart from the hard disc. Alternatively, for the purposes of this exercise, enter the small spreadsheet shown below. Then create a pie chart based on the highlighted columns. This will show the contribution to total sales made by each product.

	A	B	C	D	E
1			SALES £		
2	PRODUCT	JAN	FEB	MAR	TOTAL
3	Forks	3569.97	4376.56	4182.58	12129.11
4	Spades	4689.21	6294.34	2398.76	13382.31
5	Wheelbarrow	3693.79	4287.39	5187.17	13168.35
6	Rakes	1845.31	2398.54	397.55	4641.40
7	Secateurs	948.32	1243.98	1000.76	3193.06
8	Hoes	2389.42	2876.34	3789.99	9055.75

7 Creating an Integrated Document

Creating the Pie Chart

The pie chart is drawn as described earlier in this book, by selecting the required columns, holding down the **Ctrl** key to enable two columns to be selected simultaneously. Then the Excel Chart Wizard is used to produce the pie chart. (Please see page 122 for a fuller description).

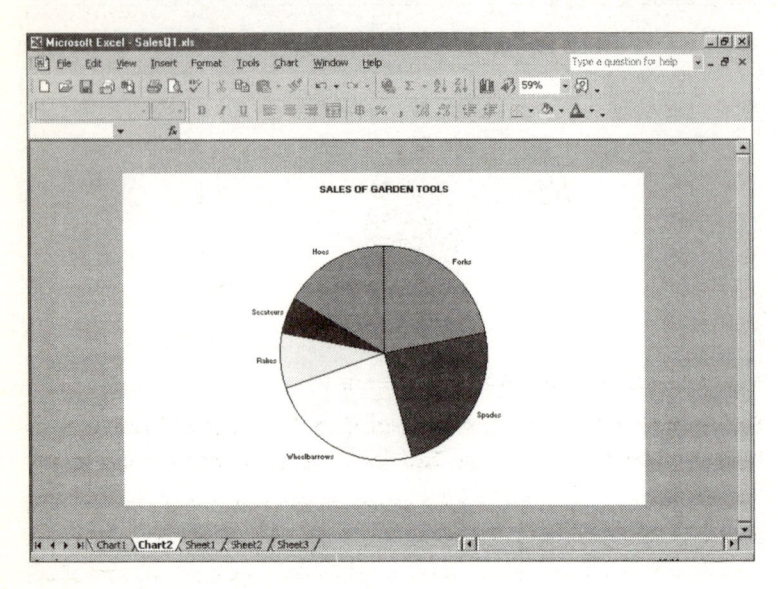

Copying the Pie Chart to the Clipboard

Select the chart by clicking anywhere in the **Chart Area** (the white rectangle containing the chart). A number of small black squares appear around the border of the Chart Area.

Select **Edit** and **Copy** to place a copy of the pie chart on the clipboard. Alternatively click the **Copy** icon on the Excel 2002 Toolbar, as shown on the left.

The clipboard contents can be viewed in the Task Pane by selecting **Edit** and **Office Clipboard...**. Alternatively hold down **Ctrl** and press the **C** key twice. The clipboard contents are shown in the Task Pane on the right of the screenshot on the next page.

Creating an Integrated Document 7

As shown below, a thumbnail of the pie chart appears in the Task Pane on the right of the Excel 2002 screen.

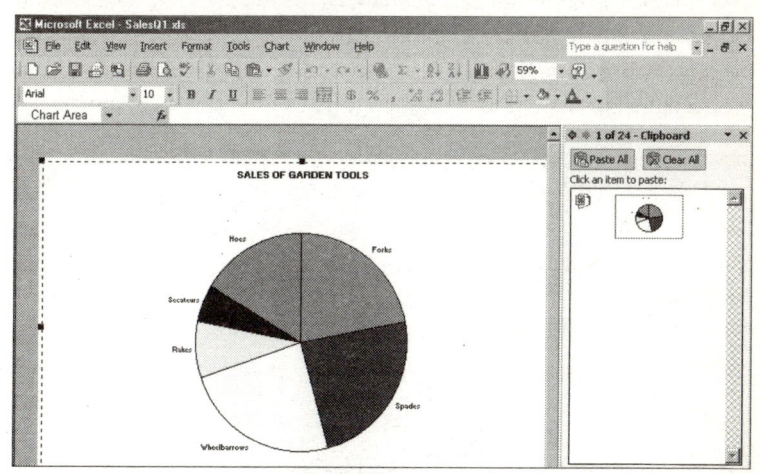

Pasting a Chart into a Word Document

Switch back to Word by clicking its icon on the Windows Toolbar or by holding down **Alt** and pressing **Tab**, then releasing when Word is listed.

The clipboard contents can be viewed in Word in the Task Pane by selecting **Edit** and **Office Clipboard...**. Alternatively hold down **Ctrl** and press the **C** key twice. Now, working within the clipboard window of the Task Pane, click the thumbnail for the chart, as shown below. The chart is pasted onto the word processor page at the insertion point.

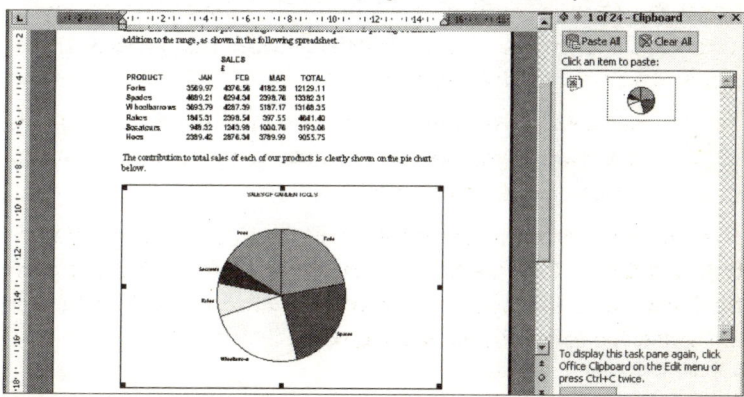

7   Creating an Integrated Document

Resizing a Chart Extract in a Word Document

Click anywhere over the chart to bring up the small black squares around the chart frame, as shown on the previous page. The chart can now be re-sized by dragging the small squares on the border.

Moving a Chart Extract in a Word Document

In order to move a chart extract about a Word document, with complete freedom and precision, it is necessary to set the *text wrapping* around the chart extract. This is done by selecting the chart, i.e. so that the small squares appear on the chart border, as shown on the previous page. Then, from the Word Menu Bar, select **Format**, **Picture…**, and click the **Layout** tab as shown below.

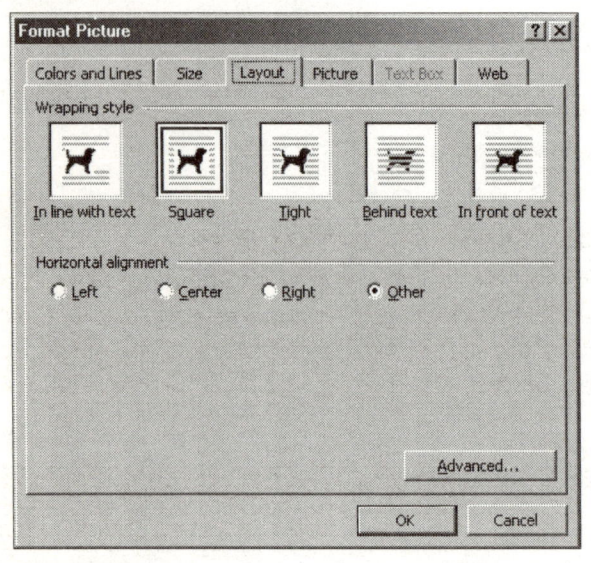

Now select a **Wrapping style** such as **Square** or **Tight**, shown above, and click **OK**. The small black squares around the border of the chart, indicating selection of the chart, immediately change to *empty circles*. Allow the cursor to hover anywhere in the chart area and the cursor changes to a cross made up of four arrows. By dragging this cross the chart extract can now be moved about the Word document with complete freedom and accuracy.

Creating an Integrated Document 7

Inserting a Database Extract into a Word Document

The following notes apply to Access 2002 database tables and queries.

Setting the Insertion Point in Word

Word 2002 should be running, with the appropriate document open on the screen. Place the cursor at the point where the top left-hand corner of the database is to be inserted, as shown below.

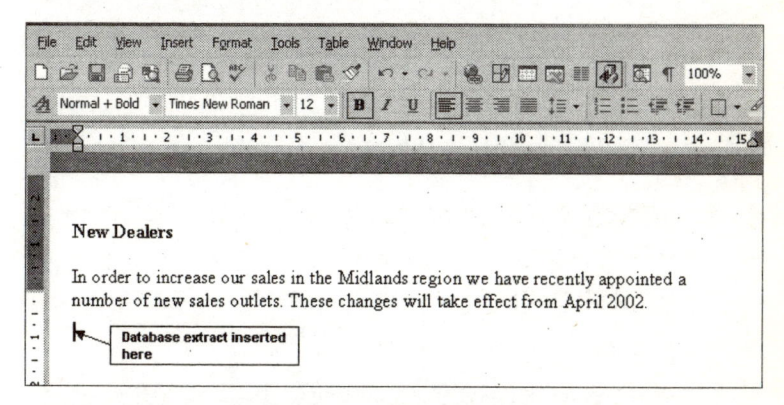

New Dealers

In order to increase our sales in the Midlands region we have recently appointed a number of new sales outlets. These changes will take effect from April 2002.

Database extract inserted here

Copying a Database Extract to the Clipboard

Now, while still running Word in the background, start the Access 2002 database, using **Start**, **Programs** and **Microsoft Access**. Open up the required database file from the hard disc. For the purposes of this exercise, you may wish to enter the short fictitious database shown below.

Name	Contact	Address	Post Code	Telephone
Birch Cross Nurseries	Mary Brown	College Lane, Marchington	BU34 9QR	01283 76594
Blue Bell Garden Centre	Barbara Faulkner	Back Lane, Rolleston-on-Dove	BU54 3JA	02036 50076
Beat All DIY	Sarah Cooper	Main St, Oundle	CR23 8RN	03353 39768
Burnaston Garden Centre	Jill Austin	Butterpot Lane, Burnaston	DE71 6NR	01332 70051
Rodsley Nurseries	Fred Greengrass	Sherwin Lane, Shirley	DE72 4KL	01873 32877
Kirk Langley Nurseries	Alice Taylor	Watery Lane, Kirk Langley	DE75 6BA	01297 60033
Hilton Hardware	Frank Tunnicliffe	Main St, Hilton	HE34 7LM	02032 30048
Hatton Stores	Roger Barker	Burton Rd, Hatton	ST45 6JN	01456 29845
Stamford DIY	John Smith	The Green, Stamford	ST54 5BY	04563 32945

7 Creating an Integrated Document

The database extract can be the entire sheet, selected by clicking the small rectangle to the left of the field names. Alternatively the extract can be just a few rows or columns, selected by clicking at the left of the row or top of the column and then dragging to highlight further rows or columns.

Now select **Edit** and **Copy** from the Access Menu Bar or click the **Copy** icon on the Access Toolbar. This places the database extract on the Windows clipboard, a temporary storage location in the computer's memory. The clipboard contents can be viewed in the Task Pane by selecting **Edit** and **Office Clipboard…**. Alternatively hold down **Ctrl** and press the **C** key twice. The clipboard contents are shown in the Task Pane on the right of the screenshot below. The entry for the database extract listed in the clipboard window of the Task pane consists of the field names and part of a record.

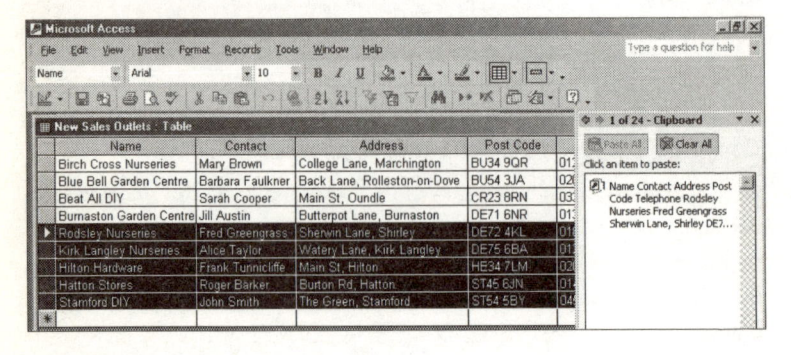

Pasting a Database Extract into a Word Document

Switch back to the Word document by clicking its icon on the Windows Toolbar, or by holding down **Alt** and pressing **Tab** then releasing the keys when Word is listed. Make sure the Word cursor is at the required insertion point for the database extract.

The clipboard contents can be viewed in Word in the Task Pane by selecting **Edit** and **Office Clipboard…**. Alternatively hold down **Ctrl** and press the **C** key twice. Now, working in the clipboard window of the Task Pane, click the entry for the database extract.

Creating an Integrated Document

The database extract is posted into the Word document at the insertion point, as shown in the lower of the two screenshots below.

Immediately after the pasting operation, the paste smart tag appears at the bottom right of the database extract, as shown on the right. This allows you to keep the original formatting of the database extract or change to a new style.

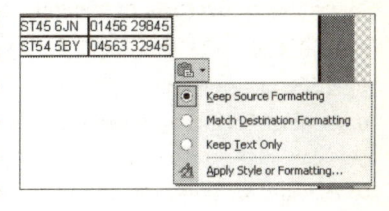

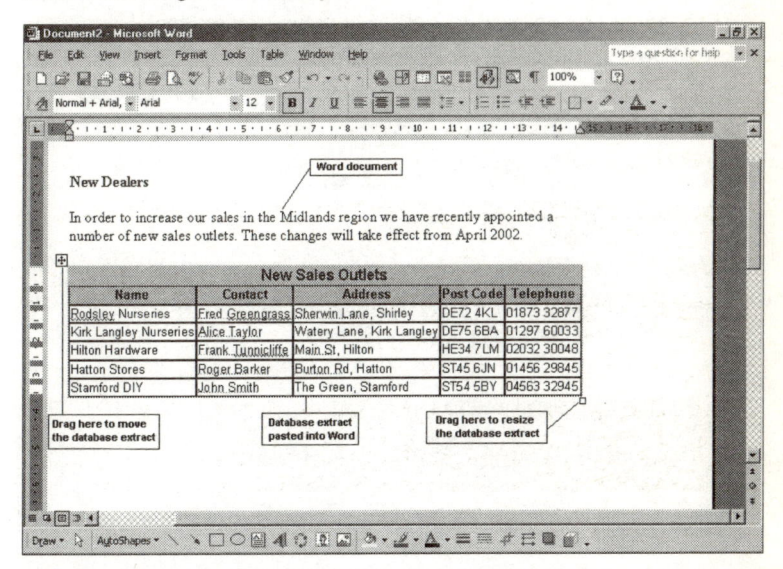

Moving a Database Extract within a Word Document

If you move the cursor inside of the database extract, a small square containing a cross appears at the top left of the extract. By dragging this square you can move the database extract into a new position, if necessary.

Resizing a Database Extract within a Word Document

When you click inside the database extract a small square appears at the bottom right. Drag this square diagonally to resize the database extract.

7 Creating an Integrated Document

Working with Pictures

Pictures can be inserted into a Word document from a variety of sources. If you require a very unusual picture or graphic, you may need to draw it yourself in a program such as Microsoft Paint, accessed by **Start**, **Programs**, **Accessories** and **Paint**. However, in many situations, ready-made *clip art* provides a convenient source of graphics. Clip art may be supplied on a CD containing several thousand graphic images to be installed on your hard disc. Alternatively, clip art collections may be downloaded from the Internet. Clip art supplied in this way is usually quite cheap or even free. Graphics images and photographs may also be copied to your hard disc via a scanner.

Microsoft Office XP allows you to organise your clip art into libraries or collections.

Inserting Clip Art into a Word Document.

Setting the Insertion Point in Word

Microsoft Word 2002 should be running with the appropriate document open on the screen. Insert the cursor at the point where the top left-hand corner of the graphic is to appear.

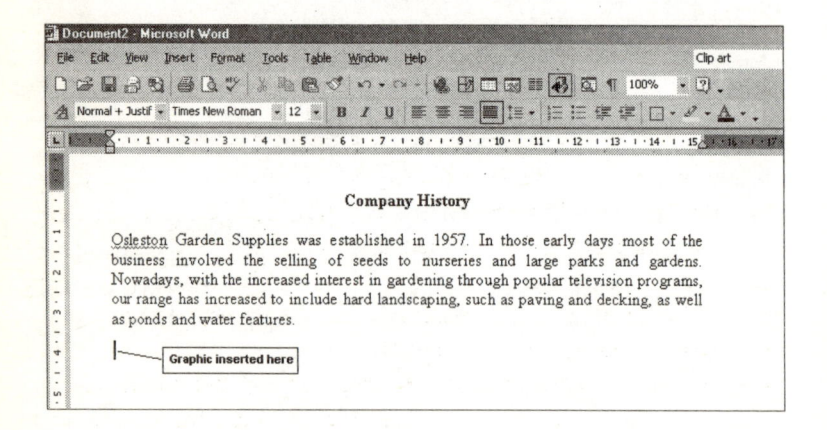

Creating an Integrated Document 7

Now select **Insert**, **Picture** and **Clip Art...** from the Word Menu Bar or click the **Insert Clip Art** icon on the Drawing Toolbar, shown right and below. (You can display the Drawing Toolbar by selecting **View**, **Toolbars** and **Drawing** from the Word Menu Bar).

The **Insert Clip Art** Task Pane now appears automatically on the right of the Word screen, as shown below.

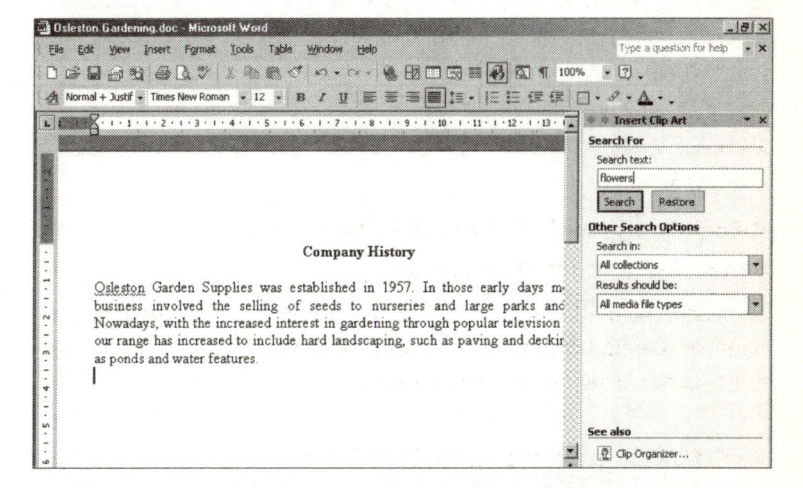

As shown in the Task Pane on the right-hand side above, there is a facility to search for clip art matching the text you type in the **Search Text:** bar. The **Search in:** drop-down menu shown right allows you to search all clip art collections (including those on the Web) or to restrict the search. Another drop-down menu under **Results should be:** allows you to search for various media types including photographs, movies and sound, as well as clip art.

167

7 Creating an Integrated Document

Any clip art images matching your search criteria are listed as thumbnail drawings in the Task Pane. Clicking the down arrow on the right of a thumbnail produces the menu shown below, which includes an **Insert** option and various options to organise your clip art.

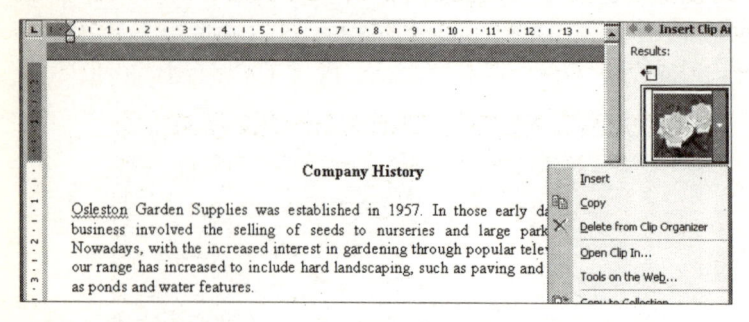

Clicking **Insert** in the menu shown above places the clip art on the Word page at the insertion point.

Inserting a Picture from a File

To insert a picture from a folder on your hard disc or perhaps from a CD or floppy disc, select **Insert** from the Word menu, then choose **Picture** and **From File....** The **Insert Picture** window opens as shown below.

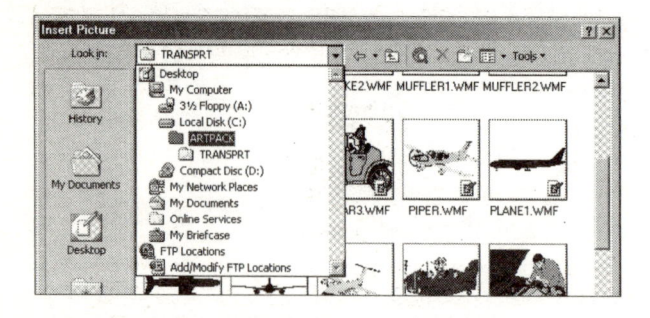

After clicking the down arrow to the right of the **Look in:** bar shown above, browse the list of discs and folders to select the required graphics image. Then click **Insert** at the bottom of the **Insert Picture** window to embed the graphic on the Word page at the insertion point.

Creating an Integrated Document 7

Moving a Graphic - Setting the Text Wrapping

In order to move a graphic freely about a page in a Word document, you need to set the *text wrapping*. First select or highlight the picture, i.e. so that several small black squares are visible around the border of the graphic. Then select **Format, Picture...**, and click the **Layout** tab. Choose a **Wrapping style** such as **Square** or **Tight**, as shown below.

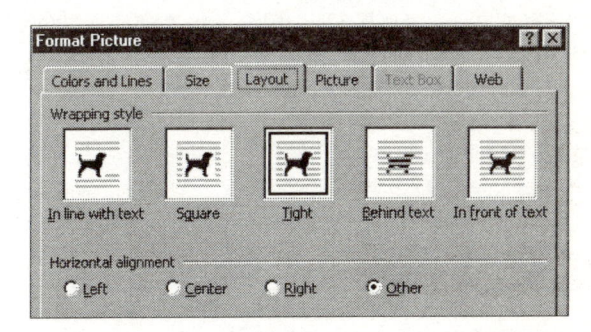

After clicking **OK** the small squares around the border of the graphic change to empty circles, as shown below. If you move the cursor over the graphic, a small cross, consisting of four arrows, appears. Drag the cross to move the graphic around the page. For very small, precise movements of the graphic, select the graphic then hold down the **Ctrl** key and press one of the four arrow keys on the keyboard.

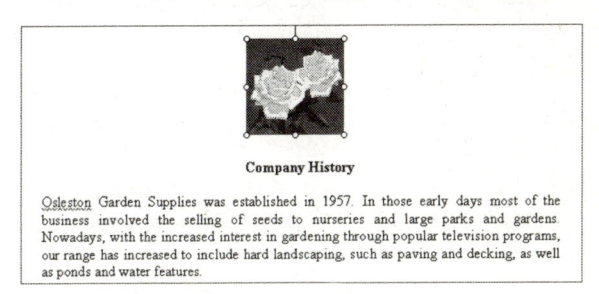

Company History

Osleston Garden Supplies was established in 1957. In those early days most of the business involved the selling of seeds to nurseries and large parks and gardens. Nowadays, with the increased interest in gardening through popular television programs, our range has increased to include hard landscaping, such as paving and decking, as well as ponds and water features.

Resizing a Graphic

Select or highlight the graphic by clicking anywhere over it. Resize the graphic by dragging one of the circles in the corners, as shown above.

7 Creating an Integrated Document

Additional Notes for the IBT II Course

The previous pages of this book have covered the basic computing skills needed by the general user of Microsoft Office 2002 and by students of CLAIT and IBT II. The following notes are intended to help students cope with some of the additional requirements of IBT II.

For the CLAIT course, students must demonstrate their ability to use computer applications such as word processors, spreadsheets, databases and software for producing graphs and charts. For each application, a separate CLAIT assignment must be completed at the computer, under controlled conditions. The CLAIT student is provided with all of the necessary raw data in explicit form - ready to be copied directly into the computer.

The IBT II course builds on the basic skills acquired in CLAIT but also requires competence in a number of other activities. IBT II students must first demonstrate ability in the use of the four main applications - database, spreadsheet, word processor and graphs and charting. The data for these IBT II assignments is not provided directly - it must be *selected* from a much wider collection of data contained on source documents. Only the specified data must be included. The data for all of the IBT II applications relates to a single realistic business situation.

The end product of the IBT II course is a single report, produced in the word processor but containing extracts from the database, spreadsheet and graphs and charting. This integrated report, including all of the extracts, must be produced to a consistent format specified in the assignment.

The IBT II course has five Elements of Certification as follows:

1. Set up and use the facilities of a database structure.
2. Create and use a spreadsheet to aid problem solving.
3. Use word processing facilities to produce a multi-page document.
4. Produce graphical representations of numeric data.
5. Integrate files and present a document.

Creating an Integrated Document

The Elements of Certification

The next few pages include listings of the IBT II Elements of Certification and the Assessment Objectives. The Assessment Objectives are the competences or skills which must be demonstrated. Many of the Assessment Objectives are also required for CLAIT and their meaning is self-evident. Others are specific to IBT II and where necessary further explanation is given.

Database

1	**Set up and use the facilities of a database structure**
1.1	SELECT the relevant data
1.2	ENTER the record structure
1.3	ENTER the data
1.4	SEARCH on three criteria to select a subset of the data
1.5	SORT data (alphanumeric/numeric)
1.6	CREATE reports
1.7	SAVE data, structure, subsets and reports
1.8	RECORD file storage details
1.9	PRINT reports

Objective 1.1 SELECT the relevant data requires the student to read through hand-written data sheets and pick out only the data specified in the assignment. For example, only enter into the database the details of those customers living in a certain area.

Objective 1.4 SEARCH on three criteria... can be accomplished in Access 2002, using a Query and by making three entries in the **Criteria:** line as shown below.

Field:	MAKE	MODEL	COLOUR	PRICE £	REG
Table:	Cars in London	Cars in London	Cars in London	Cars in London	Car
Sort:					
Show:	✓	✓	✓	✓	
Criteria:	"PORSCHE"	"911"		<20000	
or:					

7 Creating an Integrated Document

Objective 1.6 CREATE reports. Database Reports are required for IBT II and are covered on pages 87 and 88 of this book. The report is a method of presenting, in a choice of styles and layouts, an extract from a database. The report may be based on a table or a query and include all fields or a selection of fields.

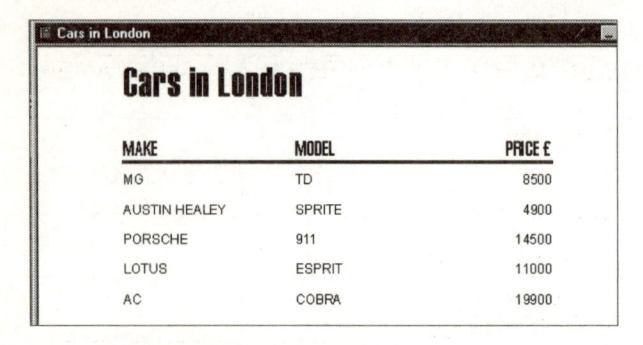

Cars in London

MAKE	MODEL	PRICE £
MG	TD	8500
AUSTIN HEALEY	SPRITE	4900
PORSCHE	911	14500
LOTUS	ESPRIT	11000
AC	COBRA	19900

Objective 1.8 RECORD file storage details. This objective is required in all of the five Elements of Certification covering the different applications - database, spreadsheet, word processing, etc. It also represents good practice in computing work in general. Basically this objective requires a record of all file names to be kept, whenever a piece of work is saved. This is because some of the files will need to be retrieved later for inclusion in the Integrated Report. The File Store Record Sheet is an essential part of the IBT II course and should be maintained and kept safe throughout the work. A copy of the File Store Record Sheet from Oxford Cambridge and RSA Examinations is shown on the next page.

Unique and Meaningful File Names

Each time the work is saved, it should be given a *unique* file name. This means that later versions of files will not overwrite earlier ones, so you will have files on disc representing all stages of the work. The files should also be given *meaningful* file names. The file name **Customers in Banbury**, for example, is more meaningful than names like **JIM1** or the default **db1** which are sometimes used. This will help to identify the file when it has to be retrieved at a later date.

IBT II ASSIGNMENTS
FILE STORE RECORD SHEET

Candidate Name:_____

ASSIGNMENT	STEP No.	FILENAME
DATABASE		
SPREADSHEET		
WORD PROCESSING		
GRAPHS		
INTEGRATION		
COPY NAME		

THIS SECTION IS FOR TUTOR USE ONLY

The Tutor should tick the assignment boxes below to indicate achievement of the Assessment Objective 'RECORD file storage details' for each assignment.

Database☐ Spreadsheet☐ Wordprocessing☐ Graphs☐ Integration☐

Copy Name☐

I confirm that I am able to recall the student's work by use of the filenames listed above.

Tutor's signature:_____

7 Creating an Integrated Document

Spreadsheet

2	**Create and use a spreadsheet to aid problem solving**
2.1	SELECT the relevant data
2.2	ENTER the spreadsheet layout
2.3	ENTER text and data into the spreadsheet
2.4	GENERATE and APPLY formulae
2.5	INSERT a column/row
2.6	GENERATE projections
2.7	SAVE structure and data
2.8	RECORD file storage details
2.9	PRINT the spreadsheet data
2.10	PRINT spreadsheet formulae

Objective 2.6 GENERATE Projections. A spreadsheet might be initially calculated using VAT at 17½%. Then the sheet might be recalculated using a value of 15%. The new, projected values must be calculated correctly and any text amended to reflect the changes.

Word Processing

3	**Use word processing facilities to produce a multi-page document**
3.1	IMPLEMENT a document format
3.2	ENTER the data
3.3	USE emphasis
3.4	USE indentation
3.5	CENTRE line(s)
3.6	PRESENT a table
3.7	NUMBER the pages
3.8	SAVE the document
3.9	RECORD file storage details
3.10	PRINT the document

Creating an Integrated Document   **7**

3.1 IMPLEMENT a document format. The following settings for the document will be specified in the assignment. (Settings given are examples only).

a	Top margin	e.g. Not less than 1.3 cm (½ inch)
b	Left margin	e.g. Not less than 1.3 cm (½ inch)
c	Line length	e.g. 16.5 cm (6½ inches)
d	Line spacing	e.g. Single
e	Justification	e.g. Justified
f	Character size	e.g 10 point
g	Paper size	e.g. A4
h	Page numbers	e.g. Bottom right. Start at page 20.

Most of the above are discussed in Chapter 6, Further Work with Word 2002. Otherwise they are covered in Chapter 2, Using Microsoft Word 2002.

Consistency of Font and Character Size

The same font and character size should be used in all of the applications, i.e. database, spreadsheet, word processor, etc. Times New Roman or Arial size 10 or 12 are suitable examples for this sort of work.

Graphs and Charts

4	**Produce graphical representations of numeric data**
4.1	SELECT the relevant data
4.2	ENTER text
4.3	PRODUCE graphical representations
4.4	SAVE the graphical representations
4.5	RECORD file storage details
4.6	PRINT the graphical representations

7 Creating an Integrated Document

Integration

5	**Integrate files and present a document**
5.1	RETRIEVE previously stored document
5.2	IMPORT information according to instructions
5.3	AMEND documents
5.4	FORMAT information
5.5	SAVE file
5.6	COPY file
5.7	RECORD file storage details
5.8	PRINT final document

Objective 5.2 IMPORT information according to instructions. This requires extracts from the Database, Spreadsheet and Graphical Representation assignments to be integrated into the word processing document. For this task an up-to-date File Store Record Sheet (as shown on page 173) is essential, in order to locate and retrieve the correct files. The extracts to be imported may be specified portions from the applications rather than entire spreadsheets or database files. An imported graphical representation extract should be re-sized to suit the document format and must be legible.

Objective 5.4 FORMAT information. The integration assignment will specify a document format of the type shown on page 175. This should be maintained throughout the entire integrated document. For example, the same font and character size should be used throughout the integrated document. Page numbers should be positioned as specified in the assignment. Page breaks should be positioned appropriately without splitting paragraphs or separating headings from related text.

Objective 5.6 COPY file. This task can be carried out in the Windows Explorer and is described in detail on page 22 of this book.

Oxford Cambridge and RSA Examinations

Checklist of Skills for IBT II

Objective	Achieved
1 Set up and use the facilities of a database structure	
1.1 SELECT the relevant data	☐
1.2 ENTER the record structure	☐
1.3 ENTER the data	☐
1.4 SEARCH on three criteria to select a subset of the data	☐
1.5 SORT data (alphanumeric/numeric)	☐
1.6 CREATE reports	☐
1.7 SAVE data, structure, subsets and reports	☐
1.8 RECORD file storage details	☐
1.9 PRINT reports	☐
2 Create and use a spreadsheet to aid problem solving	
2.1 SELECT the relevant data	☐
2.2 ENTER the spreadsheet layout	☐
2.3 ENTER text and data into the spreadsheet	☐
2.4 GENERATE and APPLY formulae	☐
2.5 INSERT a column/row	☐
2.6 GENERATE projections	☐
2.7 SAVE structure and data	☐
2.8 RECORD file storage details	☐
2.9 PRINT the spreadsheet data	☐
2.10 PRINT spreadsheet formulae	☐

7   Creating an Integrated Document

	Objective	**Achieved**

3   Use word processing facilities to produce a multi-page document

3.1	IMPLEMENT a document format	☐
3.2	ENTER the data	☐
3.3	USE emphasis	☐
3.4	USE indentation	☐
3.5	CENTRE line(s)	☐
3.6	PRESENT a table	☐
3.7	NUMBER the pages	☐
3.8	SAVE the document	☐
3.9	RECORD file storage details	☐
3.10	PRINT the document	☐

4   Produce graphical repesentations of numeric data

4.1	SELECT the relevant data	☐
4.2	ENTER text	☐
4.3	PRODUCE graphical representations	☐
4.4	SAVE the graphical representations	☐
4.5	RECORD file storage details	☐
4.6	PRINT the graphical representations	☐

5   Integrate files and present a document

5.1	RETRIEVE previously stored document	☐
5.2	IMPORT information according to instructions	☐
5.3	AMEND documents	☐
5.4	FORMAT information	☐
5.5	SAVE file	☐
5.6	COPY file	☐
5.7	RECORD file storage details	☐
5.8	PRINT final document	☐

Index

AutoCorrect Button 31
AutoFill Options 105
AutoFormat Options 112
AutoRecover Feature 33

Bar chart 120
   creating 129
Bullets and numbering 152

Cell 91
   contents 93
Character size 146
Charts and graphs 3
   displaying 125
   shading patterns 127, 131
   title 124
   wizard 119, 123
CLAIT 2, 54, 82, 118, 141
Clipboard 9
   Task Pane 40, 156
Column width 63, 93
Comparative bar chart 121, 132
Copy and Paste 8, 157, 164
Criteria for searching database 76
Currency format 57

Data types 57
Database (Access 2002) 4, 56
   column width 63
   creating 58
   editing data 66
   entering data 63
   form view 83
   reports 87
   saving 64
Decimal format 113
Deleting column (spreadsheet) 106
Deleting row (spreadsheet) 106
Design View (database) 86
Dialogue boxes 17
Displaying formulae 99

Editing a cell (spreadsheet) 96
Editing a spreadsheet 102
Entering data (spreadsheet) 97
Entering formulae (spreadsheet) 98

Field 55
File Store Record Sheet 173
File 4, 18, 19, 20, 56
Find and Replace 43
Folders 18, 19
Form
   creating 83
   design view 86
   form view 4, 83
   wizard 84
Formatting
   numbers 113
   spreadsheet 107, 108, 110
   Toolbar 49
   Word 46
Formulae (spreadsheet) 94, 98, 99
Formula Bar 95, 102
Functions (spreadsheet) 96

Go To (spreadsheet cell) 93
Graphical User Interface (GUI) 10
Graphs and charts 3, 119
Gridlines (Word tables) 152

IBT II 2, 5, 170
Importing into Word 154
   database extract 163
   graph/chart 159
   picture/graphic 166, 168
   spreadsheet extract 155
Indentation 47, 145
Inserting column (spreadsheet) 108
Inserting row (spreadsheet) 108
Integer format 114
Integration 5, 153

Keyboard shortcuts 51

Labels (spreadsheet) 93, 97
Landscape orientation 100, 126
Leader 150
Legend 123, 124, 130, 133
Line graph 121, 135
Line length 144
Line spacing 48
Longer documents 153

Index

Margins	46, 144
Measurement units	48
Microsoft	
Access 2002	4, 55
Excel 2002	3, 89
Office XP	1, 6
Word 2002	2, 25, 143
Mouse Operations	13
Multitasking	153
My Computer	14
Number format	57
Numbering pages	147
Numbers (spreadsheet)	94
Page breaks	148
Page numbers	147
Paper size	146
Paste Options	8, 41
Pasting into Word	8, 156, 157
Pie chart	120
Portrait orientation	100
Printing	44
chart	126
formulae	99
query	78
spreadsheet	99
Queries	71
saving	78
searching a file	78
sorting	73
Recalculation	89
Record structure	57
editing	63
saving	61
Record	55
deleting	69
inserting	69
Replication	98, 104
Report	87
Resizing a chart or graph	137
Saving your work	32
database	61, 64, 78
graphs and charts	126
spreadsheet	99
word processor	29, 32, 34
Search criteria	76
Searching a file	76
Selecting columns	122
Shortcut icons	23
Shortcuts, keyboard	51
Sizing a chart or graph	137
Smart Tags	6
Sorting, database query	73
Sorting, quick	75
Spell checking	42
Spreadsheet (Excel 2002)	3, 89
column width	93
creating	97
editing	102
entering data	97
formatting	110
formulae	94
SUM function	95
Table View (Database)	4
Tables (word processor)	151
Tabs	149
Taskbar	12
Task Pane	8, 40, 156
Total rows and columns	95, 103
Units	48
Vertical scale, changing	136
Windows Explorer	18
Windows Operating System	10
Windows, displaying several	16
Word processor (Word 2002)	2, 25
block operations	38
editing text	36
entering text	30
longer documents	143
screen layout	28
Wrapping (text)	162, 169